TILL FAITH

Born in 1954, Jonathan Romain graduated from University College, London in Jewish History and then gained his Ph.D. from the University of Leicester. He studied for the rabbinate at the Leo Baeck College, and since 1980 he has been the minister of Maidenhead Synagogue. During that time he has also worked extensively in the field of mixed-faith marriages, both as researcher and counsellor, and has pioneered a new approach to the subject in Britain. His previous publications have included *Signs and Wonders* (a Hebrew primer); *The Jews of England*; *I'm Jewish, My Partner Isn't*; and *Faith and Practice: A Guide to Reform Judaism Today*. With Anne Kershen, he wrote *Tradition and Change: A History of Reform Judaism in Britain 1840–1995*, while he produced *In A Strange Land* together with Bernard Kops. He contributes articles to a variety of papers and broadcasts regularly on the radio. He is married to Sybil Sheridan and they have four sons.

TILL FAITH
US DO PART

Couples who fall in love
across the religious divide

Jonathan A. Romain

Fount
An Imprint of **HarperCollins***Publishers*

Fount Paperbacks is an Imprint of
HarperCollins *Religious*
Part of HarperCollins *Publishers*
77–85 Fulham Palace Road, London W6 8JB

First published in Great Britain
in 1996 by Fount Paperbacks

1   3   5   7   9   10   8   6   4   2

A catalogue record for this book is
available from the British Library

ISBN 0 00 627925–2

Typeset by Harper Phototypesetters Limited
Northampton, England
Printed and bound in Great Britain by
HarperCollinsManufacturing Glasgow

For Doris and George
and all those who struggle with love

Contents

Preface

Doris and George – a Christian and a Jew – who have been married to each other for eight years told me that they felt they were 'the blank page between the Old and the New Testament'. They found themselves sandwiched between two traditions, part of them, but not fully at home in either. They were very much at one with each other, but wished they could feel so at ease with their respective faiths. As George put it, 'It is wonderful to have fallen in love, but God has decided not to make it easy for us.' The irony is that although they feel isolated, in fact they are not alone – they represent a significant and growing number of couples in Britain today who stem from a wide range of different religions. That blank page is occupied by so many others that it is virtually a book in itself. This book is about them and for them.

I have long been interested in mixed-faith relationships, but became actively involved in 1987 after something that took me by surprise. I organized a series of discussion evenings for members of my congregation in Maidenhead who faced particular issues. They were on bereavement, divorce, the needs of elderly parents, problems with teenage children, and intermarriage. They each attracted a good number of participants – except the latter, which had an enormous attendance, far beyond my expectations, and included many who lived a considerable distance away and had somehow heard of the event. It was clear that it was a topic that was not being tackled and was crying out for attention. Since then I have organized seminars throughout the country and met individually with several hundred couples. Their stories, problems and joys have provided much of the material for this book. I am grateful to them for their insights. It should be noted, though, that several of the names quoted in the following pages have been changed in order to avoid causing any embarrassment for them or their families.

A number of people deserve thanks for their help: Rabbi Tony Bayfield for hosting some of the seminars for mixed-faith couples at the Sternberg Centre – the headquarters of the Reform Synagogues of Great Britain – and for his encouragement over many years of working together. Naomi Berger, Pat Freeman, Wendy Greengross, Sheila King Lassman of Community Outreach have proved wonderful people with whom to work, as have many rabbinic colleagues from the Leo Baeck College. Ruth Reardon and Rev. Dr Christopher Lamb shared with me the results of the splendid work they themselves have done. Marlena Schmool (and the Board of Deputies Community Research Unit) assisted with statistical material. Brian Pearce was full of useful contacts. Dr Manazir Ahsan, Dr Zaki Badawi, Rev. Marcus Braybrooke, Deepak Naik, Indarjit Singh, and Most Venerable Pandith Vajiragnana were generous with their advice. I am also grateful to Giles Semper of HarperCollins for being so enthusiastic about the book when I first suggested it to him. My wife, Sybil, let me borrow her computer to write this, and four boys ensured I was interrupted to tie up shoelaces, play cricket and fulfil other important tasks. A special debt of gratitude is due to my own congregation, Maidenhead Synagogue, for helping to pioneer a new approach to mixed-faith couples that is welcoming and positive, and that has made a real difference to many people's lives.

Jonathan A. Romain
Maidenhead 1996

Chapter One

For better, for worse?

The issues surrounding mixed faith marriages – why
they are seen as a problem by some, enriching by
others – and the growing rate of mixed-faith marriages
today

> Where two faiths one pillow share
> Certainly the Devil is there

This medieval proverb is doubly revealing: it shows the religious and cultural hostility to mixed-faith marriages that existed in the past, and whose influence is still active today; it also demonstrates that, despite such opposition, mixed-faith marriages did occur and were regular enough for a proverb to spring up about them. But why was the Devil reckoned to be present in such unions? Was it a religious statement, because the faith of one partner was weakened and heresy entered the household? Or was it an empirical observation, because the differences between the couple caused friction and led to a troubled family life?

Today, talk of the Devil is much less common and religious vocabulary has waned in the daily speech of most people. Yet the issue of mixed-faith marriage still arouses highly emotive feelings – whether amongst the religiously committed or

1

nominal members or even those who profess not to care. Moreover, the numbers involved in such marriages have spiralled enormously in the latter half of the 20th century and it has leapfrogged over most other topics to become the most thorny problem on the agenda of a wide spectrum of faiths.

One indication of the complexity of the issue is finding the best term to describe it. The expression 'mixed-faith marriages' is used in this book as a convenient shorthand which will be intelligible to most people. However, it contains two flaws. It ignores the fact that a significant number of couples are not married but are living together. They are in a fully committed and fully consummated relationship, but not technically man and wife. This is a phenomenon affecting society at large and includes many same-faith couples, but it often applies particularly to mixed-faith ones. Lack of parental approval and unresolved question marks in the couple's own minds over the type of wedding mean that many mixed-faith couples prefer to sidestep these problems by avoiding an official marriage ceremony. As Jenny (a Catholic) put it: 'There's a sort of unwritten rule: so long as my dad can tell the rest of the family I'm not married, he will put up with Malik and me sharing a flat. If he had to say I was married to a Muslim, then life would be impossible.' Some couples are happy to go along with this arrangement and cohabit, although others are bothered by it. Gerald senses the dilemma acutely: 'Sometimes I feel as if I am living in sin, but for the time being I reckon it would be a greater sin to outrage the family by being the first member not to get married in synagogue.'

The other disadvantage with the term 'mixed-faith marriages' is that not all of the unions are mixed-faith ones. Some of them are single-faith – meaning that one partner has a faith and the other does not. In the case of the latter it may be that they were brought up in a religious tradition which they subsequently repudiated. Alternatively, they may never have received any religious orientation. The forms which hospital patients have to complete on being admitted often ask the person's religion, but a high percentage leave a blank space or simply put 'nothing'. They are not lapsed Anglican or former Jews or ex-Catholic, but simply nothing – never having been given a faith and never having taken one up of their own accord. There are those who find this hard to comprehend: 'But you must be something', Jill, a regular churchgoer, remembers telling Harry when they first met. He was not. In an age of secularism there are many who are second or third-generation 'nothings'. This can sometimes be an advantage, leaving the religious partners free to practise their own faith and introduce it in the home. However, although the problem of religious competition may not arise, religious indifference or resentment can be equally divisive. The non-religious partners may consider domestic rituals and family gatherings at festivals to be an intrusion, and resist any attempts to introduce them or to 'indoctrinate' the children.

The difficulty is that most other terms are even more inappropriate. 'Mixed relationships' may avoid the theological and matrimonial problem, but could be applied to other groupings, such as mixed-class or mixed-race. They too face many challenges, but as they can often involve people of the same faith, they must be considered a different category. The term also carries the connotation of 'mixed-up' and confused, which would be unfair on a large percentage of couples. 'Marrying out' is also an inappropriate phrase because, as will be seen below, many individuals do not feel that they are jettisoning their own religious identity by marrying someone of a different faith. The religious authorities may view it that way, but their perspective does not always match the reality of what is happening in people's lives. 'I hate that term,' Rachel said, 'it is so negative. It implies that marrying out is giving up. Falling in love with Christopher meant I loved *him*, not that I suddenly hated my religion.' Moreover, in cases where one partner does not have a faith but feels happy to go along with the other person's beliefs and practices they vehemently object to the term, as does Helen: 'It's not a matter of Harvey marrying out, but of me marrying in!'

The expression 'intermarriage' has the advantage of being short and slipping easily off the tongue, but is too imprecise. 'Exogamy' is more accurate but tends to send people scuttling for a dictionary. 'Cross-cultural marriage' draws attention to the fact that it is often the cultural expression of beliefs, rather than the beliefs themselves, that can be problematic. Thus Trudy, a Methodist, values the command to honour one's parents as much as does her Jewish husband, David. However, she finds it annoying that he feels obliged to ring his mother every day, whereas she speaks to her mother once a week. But, 'cross-cultural marriage' can also refer to a Catholic Bolivian peasant married to a Catholic Austrian countess and does not necessarily include religious differences. For the purposes of this book, therefore, 'mixed-faith marriages' is the preferred, albeit imperfect, term of reference. Others will be used occasionally, but purely for the sake of variation. The only situations that are specifically excluded are where one partner has converted to the faith of the other, in which case they are now in a same-faith marriage.

Of course, it could be argued that all marriages are mixed-faith ones. Even when people share the same religion, they may have different images of God, different ways of praying, different childhood experiences. The personality of a local priest during one's teens – sensitive or repressive, stimulating or soporific – can radically affect one's outlook and lead partners in later life to be amazed to hear each other's understanding of the same faith. Even for those with an entirely similar religious background, marriage can present some formidable challenges. The current divorce rate in Britain – one in three of all marriages – includes a high percentage of same-faith marriages and shows how precarious marriage itself can be today. There is no suggestion that same-faith marriages are automatically

4

successful and are always full of bliss and harmony.

The reality is that marriage can be wonderful or horrendous, depending on the couple, the effort they put into the relationship, and the support they receive from others. The same applies to mixed-faith marriages, only more so. The successful ones can be highly enriching, with the partners bringing together two vastly different sets of experiences and expectations that they manage to intertwine to form a new and creative household. For the unsuccessful couples, mixed-faith marriage is a minefield, with their differences jarring constantly and exploding at unexpected moments. There are also plenty of mixed-faith marriages somewhere in between these two extremes, which jog along uneventfully most of the time but face periodic crises at seasonal observances (Passover meal, Christmas Eve) or cycle-of-life moments (a birth or death in the family).

This is one of the reasons why mixed-faith marriages are such an issue, particularly from the point of view of family who watch with concern. It boils down to the simple question: will it work? There are those who may object for other reasons, but for many parents there is a genuine fear that 'marriage is hard enough at the best of times, so why add to your potential difficulties?' Alice is Jewish and was happily married to Derek (Church of England) until he died of cancer. Several years later she remarried, this time to a fellow Jew. She does not regret her first marriage in any way, save that it was cut short, but she had to admit that marrying within one's faith was much simpler. 'It's the difference between slipping into a cold bath and into a warm bath,' she said. 'One may be refreshing, but the other is so much easier and feels much more comfortable.'

A second factor that makes such marriages so contentious is the religious aspect. If you believe that your faith is the only true faith, then it is enormously painful if a member of your family – or of your flock – chooses to ally themselves with someone who does not share that faith. Even those who take a less exclusive view, and consider their faith to be but one of many paths to God, still hold its traditions precious and are dismayed at the thought that they may not be continued. Underlying these fears is the assumption that mixed-faith marriages inevitably lead to a weakening of faith. Some religious leaders have chosen to express this in extreme language, talking about 'genocide in the bedroom'. More sober commentators will point to the likelihood that at least one partner, if not both, will gradually keep less and less of their religious practices, so as not to create rifts or times of separation between them. Margaret's story bears this out. A devoted Anglican, she attended church every Sunday morning before she met her lapsed Muslim boyfriend, Mohammed, when they were both at college. Her churchgoing did not present a problem, they simply dated around it. Even after they married, it was assumed that she would go off to services. However, as their weekday jobs became very time-consuming and impinged on Saturdays too, time together on Sunday became more precious and she slowly found herself going to church less and less so that they 'didn't lose Sundays as well.'

Even if the partners manage to maintain their own religious life, it is often questioned whether the children of those marriages will receive as much religious input of one particular faith as they might have done if both parents shared that faith. 'We may not lose you,' a Catholic priest told Martin, 'but if you marry out of the faith we will almost certainly lose your children.' Churches, synagogues, mosques and other religious institutions do not just deal in ordinary time, but are also immersed in eternity. Whilst they may be involved in day-to-day details of prayers, Sunday classes and tombolas, they always have half an eye on the future and the souls of yet-unborn grandchildren. From their perspective, mixed-faith marriages can present a worrying challenge to the religious map of tomorrow, and, with some exceptions, have provoked tremendous opposition from ministers of all faiths.

The third reason that makes mixed-faith marriages such a highly-charged subject is the least savoury, and perhaps the most powerful: prejudice. It is the age-old human virus of the dislike of the unlike. It explains why so many parents who do not take their own religion seriously are aghast when their offspring marry someone from a different faith. In theory they may agree with everything that other faith stands for – loving your neighbour as yourself, giving to charity – but in practice they find themselves choking at the thought of a son or daughter-in-law from a different religious system. Bill is a practising liberal Christian, believes we are all equal in the sight of God, and has told his family so many times that 'I follow my way and let others follow theirs; the only important thing is getting on with others around you' – that they all know it off by heart. However, he turned out to be very hostile to his son's engagement to a Hindu girl. It took him several months to analyse his feelings. It was partly a matter of colour prejudice, but also resistance to a form of worship that was totally alien to anything he knew. The general tolerance he was fond of expressing verbally was found to be severely wanting when a situation arose that affected him personally. Prejudice knows few barriers and can also exist within white-white and fellow-Christian matches. Richard's parents are lapsed Protestant and never go to church, but they refused to attend his wedding to Julie, a Catholic, if it was held in her church because they do not approve of 'left-footers' (a disparaging term for Catholics) or wish to step inside their place of worship. Their attitude was not based on theology, colour or even personal antipathy, but was simply an inherited resistance, conditioned by centuries of religio-cultural indoctrination. For them and for many others, that which is different is threatening, dangerous and to be avoided. Every time that young children burn a Guy Fawkes effigy on 5th November so that the 'Catholic plot should not be forgot,' or they attend church and hear Jews described as 'a generation of vipers' (Matthew 12:34; Luke 3:7), or they learn in history lessons about noble Crusaders rescuing Jerusalem from the swarthy Muslims, then one more faggot is added to the pyre of religious prejudice and helps it keep burning for another generation.

Mixed-faith marriages have always existed and can be found throughout the world, but in modern Britain they present a particularly striking, and as yet uncharted, phenomenon. Until 1945, London was the centre of a vast empire, at whose pinnacle was the head of the Church of England, and whose subjects included nearly all the Hindus in the world, all the Sikhs, a large proportion of the Muslims and enormous numbers of Buddhists. Since then the empire has disappeared, but its former citizens have mingled extensively, many of them migrating to England. It has had a dramatic effect on the religious landscape:

◆ Within living memory every religion tended to be restricted to specific parts of the world. If one wished to see Buddhism at first hand it was necessary to travel to Ceylon or Japan. Now the Chiswick Vihara has some twenty thousand people on its mailing list, and saffron-robed monks walk the Sussex lanes or the streets of Wolverhampton. A Japanese peace pagoda rises on a lakeside in Milton Keynes and another is to tower above the suburbs of London. Muslims lived, then, in Arabia, overspilling into North Africa and eastwards into Persia and India. Now among Nash's terraces surrounding Regent's Park the great dome of a splendid mosque symbolizes the presence of nearly a million Muslims in the United Kingdom. Hindus were formerly the citizens of the Indian Empire. Now Leicester has the largest Hindu community, after Durban, outside India; and Birmingham and Wolverhampton, Manchester and Leeds, Coventry and Bristol, as well as dozens of much smaller towns, have flourishing temples ... Sikhs, too, have left their ancestral homes in northwest India ... Some two hundred thousand of these 'disciples' are now settled in Britain ... Nor should we forget the Chinese 'diaspora' scattered the length and breadth of these islands ... There are, too, small communities of

Jains, of Zoroastrians, and of Bahais ... (in addition) there are 335,000 Jews living in the UK.[1]

Rudyard Kipling may have considered that 'East is East, and West is West, and never the twain shall meet' but demographic trends have proved him wrong. If the map of Britain was to be colour-coded according to the settlement patterns of members of different faiths, it would produce a sparkling tapestry, with a rich variety of hues and shades running across each other and resembling Joseph's coat of many colours in a spin-dryer. Not only is it a multi-faith society, but it has been for over forty years. The children of those religious immigrants (and in many cases their grandchildren) have been born in Britain and have grown up in the same roads, nurseries, schools, sports clubs and jobs as other citizens. Certain voluntary ghettos may exist – Jewish areas, Hindu quarters, Muslim parts – but many have chosen to mix outside these domains, or have been forced by economic circumstances to do so. They live and work along-side members of other faiths. It is hardly surprising, therefore, that physical proximity has led to social contact and has quickly developed into sexual attraction and emotional bonds. The sheer humanity of each other has broken through the religious barriers. Jack spoke for thousands of other couples when he said, 'When I met Varda for the first time, I didn't think "Gosh, what a nice Hindu," I thought, "Gosh, what a nice person she is." ' What is surprising is that so many people – be it parents, priests, rabbis or imams – have been caught off-guard by the explosion in such relationships. In a multi-religious country such as Britain today mixed-faith marriages are inevitable. They are the price of an open society in which pluralism and tolerance are regarded as virtues. Some will regard it as too high a price to pay and seek to retreat behind ghetto walls and isolate themselves. Many will attempt to find a middle path – participating in society at large but maintaining distinctive family lifestyles, including marriage patterns. Their success rate, however, is subject to so many factors over which they have no control that it cannot be taken for granted. Others will be indifferent to the new trend and consider it a sign of a mature society that can accommodate diversity both inside and outside the front doormat.

The exact number of mixed-faith marriages is impossible to quantify as marriage licences do not specify the religion of each partner. The place of marriage itself does not provide a firm guide, for although, say, a Methodist ceremony can be taken to imply that at least one partner is Methodist, the other may be Muslim and the minister very accommodating. Indeed, some unexpected situations can occur because the law of the land requires the Church of England to marry those within its parish who request to be wed. It is possible for a Sikh to marry a Jew at the altar, with both retaining their own faith, and be registered as a Church of England ceremony. Census forms are also unsatisfactory as they do not ask questions of religious identity and so give no indication of mixed-faith households. Until recently the only information was anecdotal with ministers reporting that there was an increase in members of their flock marrying in registry offices. While some of these are same-faith couples who wish to avoid the pomp, religiosity or expense of church and synagogue weddings, many are mixed-faith couples for whom a civil ceremony presents the least amount of problems in terms of personal feelings and family dynamics. Civil marriages in 1993 accounted for 51.1% of all marriages performed that year. It was the first time that civil marriages had outnumbered religious ceremonies. Moreover the gulf between the total number of marriages taking place and the number of religious marriages is widening. In 1993, for instance, the overall total of marriages in England and Wales was 73.3% of the 1968 level, whereas the number of religious marriages was 55.6% of that level. It means that almost half of all weddings are non-religious ceremonies, and that the number is on the increase. Statistics on mixed-faith marriages are at last being drawn up by some faith-communities who are becoming alarmed at the trend. Unfortunately the largest religious organization and the one that most often performs mixed-faith weddings because of its legal obligations, the Church of England, has not yet analysed its ceremonies.

One group that has begun to collate information is British Jewry. Its findings are still at an early stage but they will serve as a useful barometer of religious patterns in general. The Jewish community has been worried by the progressive drop in its population in recent decades:

$$450,000 \text{ in } 1945$$
$$335,000 \text{ in } 1975$$
$$300,000 \text{ in } 1990$$

This has been matched by rapid decline in the Jewish marriage rate. Only half of those Jews born in the late 1950s and early 1960s who would statistically have been expected to marry in synagogues in the early 1980s actually did so. Research for more recent years indicates that only a third of the anticipated number of synagogue weddings took place.[2] There is a variety of possible factors to explain this staggering two-thirds shortfall: emigration of young people, civil marriage among Jews, non-marriage or cohabitation, and no doubt each play a part. However, the general consensus is that the major reason is marriage with a non-Jewish partner. Although no figure for the latter can be given until the overall deficit is analysed in depth, it is assumed by many that the outmarriage rate is one in three of all Jews marrying at present, if not higher. The basis for this is comparison with American Jewry, whose social and cultural patterns are very similar and where detailed research has been carried out. The outmarriage rate there shows a steep rise from the mid-1960s:[3]

Pre–1965	9%
1965–74	25%
1975–84	44%
1985–90	52%

The fact that the rate now accounts for over half of all American Jews currently getting married has had a profound psychological effect on both American and British rabbis. For the former, it meant that they could no longer claim to be holding out against assimilation as it was now clear they were losing the battle for the hearts of American Jews; for the latter, it was a shrill alarm-bell that warned 'Watch out – this is coming your way too.'

Confirmation that British Jewry as a whole is at least near such figures is found in studies of particular communities. In Grimsby, for instance, 35 of the 95 members of the Jewish community who married between 1945 and 1985 married non-Jewish partners: i.e. 37%.[4] Perhaps even more revealing for future trends is a survey taken in 1970 of Jewish students at the University of Oxford, who can be assumed to be amongst the brightest products of British Jewry and potential future leaders. 26% of them thought outmarriage 'desirable' and 52% were neutral on the issue. Only 22% were opposed to it.[5] By 1993 a broader survey of Jewish men between 20 and 35 years showed a similar result, when 53% said that they had married or would consider marrying someone of another religion. It was the clearest possible signal of the collapse in the practical and intellectual resistance to mixed-faith marriage as a stigma to be avoided at all costs.[6]

Compared to other major faiths, it is perhaps to be expected that a high percentage of Jews in Britain would marry out of the faith. This is partly because, apart from Catholics, they have been settled in Britain the longest, with the community dating back to 1656. (Jews had lived in England earlier but had been expelled by Edward 1 in 1290 and were largely absent from these shores for the intervening centuries.) It is also the case that the majority of them are white-skinned and so, despite other problems, are not victims of colour prejudice and have integrated into society without that handicap. Another reason is that although their high profile in the retail and entertainments industries leads many to grossly overestimate their numbers, the actual number of Jews is very small. Many of that number are scattered in different parts of the country, while even those that are concentrated together are never in the majority. Golders Green in north London may be referred to as 'Golda's Green' – affectionately by some, disparagingly by others – but proportionally Jews form no more than two out of five of the population. For nearly all Jews, therefore, the vast majority of their neighbours are non-Jews, and fences are as little protection against relationships developing as they are at stopping footballs flying overhead.

Calls for a full-scale survey of the entire Jewish community have not yet met with a positive response, with the time and cost involved usually being cited as a prohibitive obstacle. However, if mixed-faith marriages threaten the future of the community as much as is claimed by religious leaders, then it would seem obvious that the first step for those seeking to reverse the trend would be to establish its true nature and extent. Indeed, it has been suggested that some people may prefer not to have the figures revealed lest they prove even worse than expected and encourage others to follow suit. Like a person with toothache fearful of visiting the dentist because of worries over what he might say, British Jewry has plenty of anxious leaders who bewail the future without knowing what is really happening at present.

The mixed-marriage issue is not limited to Jews in the English-speaking world. In the rest of Europe, it is generally higher: in Paris, the rate is hovering around 50%, in Switzerland 60%, while in Denmark it is over 75%. In Germany, despite the strained relations between Jews and Germans in the wake of the Holocaust, it is 80%. In Russia it is 73%, although the suppression of Jewish education and culture by the Communists for several decades offers a different explanation for the figure. It is little wonder that Jonathan Sacks, the Chief Rabbi of Orthodox Jews in Britain, recently posed a question to Jews world-wide: 'Will we have Jewish grandchildren?' The implication was that, unless there was a radical move to shore up Jewish identity, and in particular to encourage Jews to marry *within* the faith, the future of the Jewish people could not be guaranteed. This is why the Jewish community is leading the search for accurate information on mixed-faith marriage: because whereas no religion wishes to lose a third or more of its membership, most others are numerically large enough to sustain such losses. In the case of the Jews, they are such a small group already that defections of that magnitude could almost spell the end of the faith. The fear is that outmarriage could be 'the kiss of death' and achieve in one generation what Hitler and other anti-Semites had failed to do in centuries of persecution.

The fears of British Jewry may be the most documented, but they are not unique. The Catholic Church in Britain is also concerned at what is happening to its flock. In the 1950s it was estimated that 33% of weddings under their auspices involved a Catholic marrying a non-Catholic. By the 1980s the figure had risen to 65%.[7] If one adds to that figure the Catholics who marry out of the faith in a registry office ceremony – whose number is unknown but who surely exist – then the overall rate must be even higher. The attitude of the Church to mixed-faith marriage has become more liberal in recent years, but the following official statement reveals the hostility that it provoked before that change: 'The Church firmly opposes marriages between Catholics and non-Catholics ... the majority are lost to the faith ... we can only pray that God will be merciful to them on their death-bed.'[8] The threat is clear: marry out and you are liable to go to hell. For committed

Catholics, or even those now lapsed but still fearful of the perils of damnation indoctrinated in their childhood education, it is an awesome choice: lose the person you love or forfeit your place in heaven. Whilst the figures show that many prefer the call of the present to the rewards of eternity, it is at a high cost. It produces a schizophrenic relationship with the Church – feeling attached to it yet knowing they are acting in disobedience. For some, the result is the existence of a constant tension, with a permanent sense of guilt that is unhealthy for the person concerned and that can also have a damaging effect on the marriage. As John said with obvious sadness, 'When I think about it, I feel I have let everyone down – Jesus, the saints, my priest. My wife says she understands but I don't think a non-Catholic can ever really appreciate what it is like to go against the Church. I try not to think about it too often or I will mess up my home life too.' For others, the friction between loving one's partner and loving one's faith proves too great and leads to a break with the Church. For Catharine, the crunch point came after ten years of marriage:

◆ I tried to reconcile my marriage and my faith for a long time and was determined not to give up either. But when I kept on being told that I was a sinner and that my marriage was not welcome in the sight of God I had to make a choice. Although it was a very painful moment, it was inevitable which way I would go. I knew my marriage was full of love and charity and kindness, and there was nothing unChristian about it at all. If the Catholic Church chose to deny it, then I would not. I actually live a few hundred yards down the road from my local church, but now it feels like a million miles away.

If mixed-faith marriages have important consequences both for the faith-communities and for the individuals involved, they also raise large questions affecting society in general. They are a particular issue when the social order is against such marriages. This can occur in at least three different situations. First, in a society that is largely religious and which feels threatened by a process of secularization. Mixed-faith couples are seen as fomenting change by breaking down traditional barriers. The couples themselves may still value their own religious traditions, but their circumstances may force some of them to turn into campaigners for secular developments, such as civil marriages or non-denominational cemeteries. In Israel, for instance, Jews and Muslims who wish to marry have to travel abroad – usually a day trip to Cyprus – in order to wed. Many in such relationships have found themselves joining forces with secular elements in Israel who are pressing for the legalization of civil marriages for entirely different reasons of their own. The second scenario is the challenge the mixed-faith couples pose to more authoritarian societies in which inherited identity is taken for granted. By marrying outside the group into which they were born and by fashioning a new identity with their partner, they can cause anxiety amongst conservative circles. Even more tremors are caused by the position of their children, who may belong to no established group and who can be seen as creating an unwelcome pool of people without proper structure or orientation. This can apply on a macro or micro level: to countries as a whole, or to localized areas such as a rural village in Cornwall or Kurdistan where strong local traditions persist. The third context is when mixed-faith couples are seen as flouting the political divisions in society or ignoring historic rivalries, such as Catholics and Protestants in Northern Ireland, Sikhs and Hindus in the Punjab, or Copts and Muslims in Egypt. In these situations, mixed-faith couples confront not only matters of doctrine but also issues of blood and soil and hegemony. By crossing the religious frontiers, the couple are seen as 'selling out to the enemy' and can provoke fatal consequences.

In mainland Britain today, a different challenge is posed by mixed-faith relationships: having recently become a multi-faith society, will there be a loss for everyone if ancient cultures fragment and lose their distinctive traditions? Can society encourage a breakdown of the barriers of ignorance and mistrust that exist between particular groups, yet also allow them to maintain their distinctive identities? Will a 'religious meltdown' produce a new generation that lacks the family structures and social values promoted by the faith-communities? The search for individual happiness that leads to an age of mixed-faith marriages may also produce a collective instability that creates a more vulnerable society. Or, more positively, will it result in fewer barriers and an even more open society in which differences are celebrated rather than feared? Might there even be a quasi-messianic appeal to a development which brings diverse people together and through which religious insights are swopped and cultural expressions are shared? There is no denying the enormous contribution made by each of the major faiths, but might it be better for society at large if men and women were no longer labelled by their separate faiths but were to become part of a religious rainbow? There may also be a path in between these two extremes, in which individuals are able to marry outside their faith yet maintain their own religious heritage, respect that of their partner and transmit one or both to their children. According to this view, society is served best by encouraging those who enter mixed-faith marriages to let their traditions live on and co-exist in the same household. Would it not be a fitting fulfilment of all the ideals of love and brotherhood espoused by religions if their members turned their own homes into havens of harmony and translated the theories of religious goodwill into the practicalities of everyday life?

Notes

1 *Towards a Theology for Inter-Faith Dialogue*, London, Anglican Consultative Council, 1988, p. 4

2 Waterman, Stanley and Kosmin, Barry, *British Jewry in the Eighties*,

London, Board of Deputies of British Jews, 1986, p. 12; *The Jewish Chronicle*, London, 12 February 1993

3 Mayer, Egon, *1990 National Jewish Population Survey*, New York, Council of Jewish Federations, 1991. In some cities, the rate is as high as 70%, e.g. Denver, Colorado and Phoenix, Arizona

4 Gerlis, Daphne and Leon, *The Story of the Grimsby Jewish Community*, Grimsby, Humberside Leisure Services, 1986, p. 89

5 Wasserstein, B., 'Jewish Identification amongst Students at Oxford,' *The Jewish Journal of Sociology*, vol. XIII (1971) pp. 135–51

6 *The Jewish Chronicle*, London, 24 September 1993

7 Kelly, George, *The Catholic Marriage Manual*, London, Robert Hale, 1958, p. 160; *Interchurch Families,* Association of Interchurch Families no. 12, London, Winter 1984–5

8 Kelly, op. cit. p. 160

Chapter Two

Man proposes, religion opposes

The attitude of Judaism, Christianity, Islam, Hinduism,
Sikhism and Buddhism towards mixed-faith marriage,
and the changing responses in recent years

'Love your neighbour as yourself' (Leviticus 19:18; Matthew
22:39). These words have been preached from countless
pulpits by Christian and Jewish ministers for generations and
are taken to refer to all people, including those of a different
faith. However, it is clear that they understood this to mean
kind thoughts and good deeds only, and nothing more
personal. They are becoming increasingly shocked, therefore,
at the members of their flock who interpret those words more
literally: who not only love their different-faith neighbour out
of religious duty, but fall in love and become involved with
them emotionally and sexually. That sort of love was never
envisaged in the sacred texts.

Examination of the written sources of the major faiths
reveals outright opposition to mixed-faith marriage in some
and a more open attitude in others. The Hebrew Bible makes it
clear right from the start that same-faith marriages are the most
desirable. The first Jew, Abraham, gives explicit instructions to
his chief servant about finding a suitable wife for his son Isaac:

19

none of the local pagan Canaanites will suffice; he must select one from Abraham's former country and from his family.[1] It is an attitude that in turn is inculcated into Isaac, for he is greatly upset when his older son Esau marries local women and he urges his younger son Jacob not to do likewise.[2] The reason is assumed to be obvious and is only spelt out later in the Book of Exodus when a legislative code is laid down: 'Be careful not to … marry your sons to their daughters, and when their daughters go wantonly after their gods, they may lead your sons astray too.[3] Put bluntly, mixed-faith marriages lead to religious pollution. Further on, in Deuteronomy, this ban is extended to Israelite females marrying out, although the prohibition as a whole is limited to the seven Canaanite nations amongst whom the Israelites then lived. It is unclear whether this was because there were no other potential non-Israelite partners envisaged then, or because it was felt that women from foreign countries would be assimilated into the majority Hebrew culture and would pose no religious threat.[4]

It is obvious from a host of other references that the Israelites did marry women from other faiths – including members of the religious hierarchy, such as Moses, whose wife Zipporah was the daughter of a Midianite priest.[5] In general, however, the Bible voices its disapproval, implicitly or explicitly: when an Israelite is found guilty of blasphemy, we are told that he is the product of a mixed marriage, as if by way of explanation. When an over-zealous priest kills an Israelite man who had established a relationship with a Midianite woman, he is regarded as a national hero.[6] The condemnation reaches its climax with the arrival of Ezra in Jerusalem, bringing with him the Jews who had been exiled in Babylon. He is horrified to discover that many of those who had remained in Israel had married non-Jews and he orders them to divorce their wives. His colleague, Nehemiah, adopted a more violent approach: 'I argued with them and reviled them, I beat them and tore out their hair.' He was particularly shocked by the impact of the marriages on the children and the fact that half of them could not even speak Hebrew.[7]

The fear that characterized the Biblical pronouncements, of the damaging religious effect which the other partner may have, was to influence subsequent Christian, Jewish and Muslim teachings. In the New Testament, Paul takes a relaxed attitude to those who adopt the faith but whose partners do not convert. Unlike Ezra he does not demand they separate; on the contrary, he suggests it may even be an opportunity to redeem the non-believer and any children they have:

◆ If a Christian has a heathen wife, and she is willing to live with him, he must not divorce her; and a woman who has a heathen husband willing to live with her must not divorce her husband. For the heathen husband now belongs to God through his Christian wife, and the heathen wife through her Christian husband. Otherwise your children would not belong to God, whereas in fact they do. If on the other hand the heathen partner wishes for a separation, let him have it. In such cases the Christian husband or wife is under no compulsion; but God's call is a call to live in peace. Think of it: as a wife you may be your husband's salvation; as a husband you may be your wife's salvation.[8]

However, this tolerance only exists with regard to existing marriages. Paul is adamantly opposed to Christians contracting marriages with non-Christians:

◆ Do not unite yourselves with unbelievers; they are no fit mates for you. What has righteousness to do with wickedness? Can light consort with darkness? Can Christ agree with Belial, or a believer join hands with an unbeliever?[9]

In his Letter to the Ephesians, Paul puts the case more positively and gives theological justification for marrying only a fellow believer: Christians are living parts of the Church, which is the body of Christ, and so they are also part of Christ's body.

At the same time, when a man and a woman marry they become one flesh. If they share the same faith, there is a perfect unity of flesh, both with each other and with the body of Christ. If they do not share the same faith, this unity is broken and the spiritual at-oneness will not be fulfilled.[10] Writing at the end of the second century, Tertullian laid down his vision of the ideal Christian marriage in which shared belief was the bedrock and allowed no room for compromise:

◆ A single faith, a single hope, a single way of life, a single service: they both serve the one Master, pray together, fast together, they instruct, exhort and help each other. They both approach the Lord's table together.[11]

The opposition to marriage outside the Church intensified with the edicts of the Church Fathers, much of whose energy was directed at fighting disbelief and internal heresies. Part of their campaign was to minimize contact with non-believers, whose influence they feared could undermine the tenets of Christian teachings. At that time, Judaism was regarded as one of the greatest dangers to the purity of the faith. Marriage between Christians and Jews was banned by the Council of Elvira in 306. The Council of Orleans (538) spelt out the penalties involved:

◆ We prohibit all Christians from marrying Jews. If they do so, no matter who they are, let them be banished from their community and have their possessions confiscated. Likewise we forbid Christians to attend Jewish celebrations. If by any chance they are proven to have attended such events, they will be forced to suffer a year's excommunication for committing a sin of this nature.

The decree set the pattern for subsequent legislation adopted throughout the Middle Ages. The fact that it needed to be repeated often indicates that it was breached often. Among the drastic steps adopted by the Church in order to strengthen the ban was the imposition of the 'Jew badge' which was promulgated by Pope Innocent III at the Lateran Council of 1215. Henceforth all Jews had to wear a distinctive item of clothing – in some countries it was a pointed hat, in England it was a piece of cloth depicting the two tablets of the Ten Commandments and sewn to one's outer garb. The idea was to distinguish Jews physically so that Christians could avoid mixing with them unawares. It was a form of religious apartheid and was to be followed in the sixteenth century by the institution of the ghetto to carry physical segregation one step further. At root, however, there was a certain logic: recognizing that what starts as a friendly chat in the street between a man and a woman of different faiths can end up as an intimate relationship, and that the only way of stopping it is to prevent the conversation even beginning in the first place. Other Christians, such as the Amish, have adopted the same principle in reverse and isolated themselves. By living in their own villages and by wearing clothing that differentiates themselves from others, they have formed voluntary ghettos as a deliberate strategy of preserving their faith.

It is clear, however, that despite all the efforts in the Middle Ages to stop them, Christians and Jews did form liaisons, including members of the clergy. In 1222, a deacon in Oxford married a Jewess, converted to Judaism and was burnt at the stake as a result. A similar fate befell the Dominican friar, Robert of Reading, after he fell in love with a Jewish woman in 1274. With such episodes as these regularly scandalizing the Church, it meant that Sir Walter Scott's fictional story, *Ivanhoe*, in which a Crusader and a Knight Templar both fall in love with a Jewish maiden, was far from fanciful. The Crusades were themselves a direct response to the rise of Islam – another threat in the eyes of the Church, who feared not only its military conquests but its religious influence. It was no coincidence that southern Spain, where the two faiths met in Europe, was renowned as a hotbed of rational philosophy in the thirteenth century and it quickly became one of the targets of the Spanish Inquisition. Muslim-Christian marriages also carried the stigma of colour difference. Shakespeare's Othello may have lacked historicity, but the sentiments expressed in it faithfully reflected the prejudices of seventeenth-century Christian England:

> Even now, now, very now, an old black ram
> Is tupping your white ewe

> ... you'll have your daughter cover'd with a Barbary horse; you'll have your nephews neigh to you; you'll have coursers for cousins and gennets for Germans.[12]

The advent of the Reformation meant that religious confrontation now occurred within the Christian world. The Catholic Church fought strenuously to protect its flock against the lure of other denominations, seeing little difference between the theological appeal of their doctrines and the sexual appeal of their members. Marriage with a person baptized in the wrong church was regarded in the same light as marriage with a non-believer. This attitude was maintained up to the twentieth century: the Catholic Church's new Code of Canon Law of 1918, *Codex Iuris Canonici*, states: 'The Church everywhere most severely forbids the contracting of marriages between two baptized persons of whom one is a Catholic whereas the other is a member of a heretical or schismatical sect.' The hostility was mutual. The religious divide was enforced by parliamentary legislation in Protestant England: under the 1726 Felony Act of George I, Catholic priests were liable to execution if they officiated at mixed-faith marriages, while a member of the royal family who married a Catholic would lose the right to the throne. The former law has been repealed, but not the latter, and it has served to maintain historic prejudices against Catholics into modern times. The Protestant Churches,

too, sustained the antipathy: a resolution...
Missouri Synod in 1953 declared that 'Ma...
Protestants and Roman Catholics is diametrically...
the eternal truths of God.' Five years later the...
Church 'earnestly warned' its members against con...
marriages with Catholics, while the Presbyterians...
instructed not to marry 'infidels, papists, or other idolaters...
The turning point came in 1962 with the Second Vatican
Council, presided over by Pope John XXIII. It revolutionized
relations between Catholicism and other Churches as well as
with other faiths. One of the many radical changes that
resulted was publication of the regulations *Motu proprio
Matrimonia Mixta* in 1970 which revised, indeed overturned,
many of the prohibitions and limitations imposed by the *Codex*
with regard to marrying other Christians. Among the main
differences were:

Codex: marriage outside of the Catholic faith is severely
forbidden, although dispensations can be given if strict conditions
are observed

Matrimonia Mixta: marriage outside of the Catholic faith is
discouraged

Codex: there is no distinction between marrying a baptized non-
Catholic and a non-Christian

Matrimonia Mixta: the distinction is acknowledged

Codex: Catholics must promise to work for the conversion of their
partner and to bring up any children as Catholics

Matrimonia Mixta: the former is not necessary, while the latter is
modified, so that if the partner objects, the Catholic is not obliged
to pursue it

take place in a Catholic church and
te

ng can take place in either church
-officiate

faith marriages, the new regula-
urden of trying to convert their
ll-feeling if they pursued it too
f they neglected to do so. For
dered discussions with their
about the wedding ceremony
and the upbringing of children free from the strictures that had
caused much heartache and resentment to previous couples. A
further change to the regulations took place in 1990 when the
Bishops' Conference of England and Wales authorized a significant alteration to the promise that Catholics had to make
before the Church would consent to a mixed marriage. The
Revised Directory stated not only that the promise could be
made verbally rather than in writing, but the new text read:

◆ I declare that I am ready to uphold my Catholic faith and to avoid
all dangers of falling away from it. Moreover, I sincerely undertake
that I will do all that I can within the unity of our partnership to
have all the children of our marriage baptized and brought up in
the Catholic Church.[14]

The key phrase was 'within the unity of our partnership' which
indicated, firstly, that the Church recognized there were limits
to what one partner in a marriage could do if the other partner
objected and so the Catholic spouse was exonerated of blame if
attempts to bring up the children as Catholic failed; secondly,
that preserving the harmony of the marital relationship was
more important than ensuring the Catholic education of the
children, and that the latter should not be done at the expense
of the former. The priority had shifted quietly but subtly to a

happy home rather than a Catholic one.

The position of the Church of England had always been much more open to those in mixed-faith marriages – although by accident rather than by design. As mentioned in the previous chapter, the law of England provides that every person resident in a parish has a right to be married in the parish church according to the rites and ceremonies of the Church of England. The only exceptions are where one party is divorced and has a previous partner still living. If the incumbent or priest-in-charge objects to the marriage for any reason, he is not obliged to conduct the marriage himself, but he must arrange for another Anglican minister to do so and allow the use of the parish church. The legislation was framed at a time when it was assumed that requests for church marriage would be from baptized Christians and so no conditions were made as to their religious affiliation. As a result, the right to a church marriage applies to everyone, whether or not they are baptized, and whether or not they belong to another faith. Thus mixed-faith couples who wished to have a church wedding have always been able to do so, and even if the resident minister found it against his conscience, another minister was procured for them. However, the same legislation that allowed this freedom also limited the type of service that was permitted. When the ring is given by the man to the woman, it is laid down in the 1662 *Book of Common Prayer* and subsequent authorized alternative services that the Trinitarian formula is used and that the marriage is conducted 'in the name of the Father and of the Son and of the Holy Ghost'. For a mixed-faith couple, this may prove unacceptable to the non-Christian partner or to their family. Unlike all other Christian denominations, the liturgy of the Church of England is prescribed by law and if this phrase is omitted, the ceremony could be deemed invalid and the legality of the marriage would be in question.

In recent years, the Church of England has been moved by

the growth in requests for marriage by mixed-faith couples to re-examine its position. Guidelines issued in 1992 urged ministers to give full pastoral support to such couples and be sensitive to their needs and backgrounds. For legal reasons mention of the Trinity could not be deleted from the service, while it was also felt that the Church would be untrue to itself if it divested the ceremony of any Christian character. However, it was suggested that additional material could be introduced to the service that was meaningful to the couple or that derived from the faith of the non-Christian partner, assuming that it was in consonance with Christian teaching. It was also recognized that for mixed-faith couples who could not subscribe to the set liturgy, it might be more appropriate to have a civil marriage to fulfil the legal requirements but then have a service of blessing in church afterwards. As the service of blessing is not controlled by Act of Parliament, the officiating ministers have much greater freedom of manoeuvre. If they wish, they can virtually compose the format from afresh, taking into account the religious diversity of the couple. References to the Trinity, or even to Jesus Christ, can be omitted, and neutral expressions can be used instead, such as 'in the name of God'.[15]

The Non-conformist churches in Britain have never been subject to legal obligations as to the complete text of their liturgy. The Methodists, for instance, responded to the change in marriage patterns by drawing up new regulations in 1974. These permit certain omissions in the wedding service, including mention of the Trinity if the non-Christian partner cannot say it in good conscience. This does not invalidate the legality of the marriage providing certain other sentences, which do not present religious difficulties, are recited. A service of blessing is another option, although the Methodist custom is to hold them in the home rather than in church.

Despite the liberalization of procedures in all the major Christian denominations in recent years, there is still resistance by certain members of the clergy to marriages with non-

Christians. What the leadership prescribes can be slow in perco-
lating down the religious hierarchy and taking root among the
parishes. Some couples have reported a distinct unhelpfulness
when approaching their local minister. Nigel, a baptized
Anglican who attends services every now and then, said:

◆ I have known the minister for years, and we often exchange a
brief word in the High Street. I expected him to quiz Rani a little
over her Hindu faith, but I was really taken aback by how hostile he
was. She ended up in tears and I could not possibly ask her to have
a church wedding after what happened.

Couples who persevere and approach another minister will
often find a much more welcoming approach. According to
Sonia:

◆ Father Pat was brilliant. He understood the problems we faced
and made everything as easy as possible for us. We are just lucky
that we made the effort to try again after the first awful experience
we had.

In this respect, Britain has been fortunate in the positive lead
shown by its bishops. A more negative stance is still in evidence
elsewhere. Canon 5b of the Church of Ceylon holds that 'The
marriage of a Christian with a non-Christian is contrary to the
teaching of Holy Scripture and to the rule of the Church' and
forbids any minister to participate. In Germany, there has been
a high increase of Christian-Muslim marriages, owing to the
growing presence of Turkish migrant workers. The 526 cases
recorded in 1965 leapt to 3,765 in 1980, a sevenfold increase
in only fifteen years. The alarm felt by some led the Bishop
of Munster, Mgr Reinhard Lettmann, to warn German
Protestants against marrying Turkish migrants:

◆ Mentalities, customs and habits are too different between the
two religions ... The difficult integration of Germans in large

29

Muslim families, the pressure of society from the father's country of origin, are amongst the distinct cultural traits.[16]

The bishop concluded by advising priests under his authority 'to have some serious talks' with those contemplating marriage to a Muslim. It was a message that may well have had an element of racism mixed with its religious objections, but it does at least have the merit of being forthright about a view shared by some Christian ministers in Britain that they feel too embarrassed to express in the current climate of inter-faith camaraderie.

When Jewish tradition sought to apply the Biblical teachings against mixed-faith marriages, the text of Deuteronomy initially presented a problem. The ban was specifically against members of the seven Canaanite nations – but by the first century there were no Hittites or Girgashites left any more, whereas there were many others whom trade and migration had brought into close proximity. Did that mean that it was permissible to marry Phoenicians or Carthaginians? Many individual Jews decided for themselves and mixed-faith marriages were a constant feature of Jewish life, particularly in the three centuries before and after the Christian era. It sometimes reached the highest levels, as in the case of Manasseh, brother of the High Priest, who had taken a non-Jewish wife. When asked to choose between giving up either her or the priesthood, he left Jerusalem and established his own Temple on Mount Gerizim in Samaria. Clarification of the law was urgently needed. As the original injunction was to prevent Jews being enticed by idolatry, the rabbis therefore ruled that the prohibition extended to all Gentiles and that any union with a non-Jew was not legally valid.[17] A series of other regulations was gradually introduced to enforce the ruling: non-Jewish partners could not be buried in a Jewish cemetery, the daughter of a Jewish woman and non-Jewish man was Jewish but considered tainted and unable to marry a priest.

In the Christian era, the ban was aided by the equal antipathy of the Church to mixed-faith marriages, so that any would-be mixed-faith lovers found themselves condemned and ostracized on all sides. As there was no such thing then as neutral territory, with society divided along religious lines into different faith-communities, any such unions could only survive if one partner converted to the other faith. The severe punishments that were visited on a Christian who converted to Judaism in many European countries, including the death penalty, meant that the marriage could only survive if it was the Jewish partners who converted. They too faced painful consequences – being subject to a *herem* (excommunication) which cut them off from all social contact with the Jewish community and being disowned by their family. In the Middle Ages there developed the custom of 'sitting *shivah*' for apostates – whereby the family would officially sit in mourning for a member who converted out of the faith, considering them dead and regarding themselves as bereaved.

The religious wall between Jews and Christians suffered a major breach with the French Revolution. Its message of liberty, equality and fraternity sought to abolish the categorization of people according to their class or faith, and to treat everyone as an individual. Napoleon not only tore down the ghetto walls that kept Jews apart physically from other French citizens, but sought to end the mutual suspicion that separated them mentally. In 1806 he summoned a Sanhedrin – a large group of rabbinic and lay leaders representing French and Italian Jewry. The twelve questions he set them concerned the relationship of Jews to the state and fellow Frenchmen, and included one asking whether they could intermarry. The representatives were in a quandary: they were grateful for the many rights given to Jews by the French Revolution, were aware that Napoleon wished to have an answer in the affirmative, and did not wish to appear racist. Yet they also felt they could not depart from tradition. The result was that they pointed out that rabbinic law was opposed to mixed-faith marriage and that such unions were not considered valid religiously in Jewish eyes. However, they did concede that mixed-faith marriages were valid civilly, acknowledged that a Jew who married a non-Jew did not lose his Jewish status, and declared that no curse or *herem* would be brought upon the person.

The response of the Napoleonic Sanhedrin typified the dilemma of Jewish authorities worldwide, who were delighted at the freedom from discrimination and persecution brought by emancipation, yet fearful of the effect it would have on communal life and maintenance of the faith. In some instances it led to drastic decisions: thus when Napoleon marched on Russia and asked the help of the Jewish population, promising to free them from the tyranny they suffered, one of the leading Hasidic rabbis, Shneur Zalman of Lyady, urged his followers to support the Tsar on the grounds that being repressed and segregated was more likely to keep Jews Jewish than being liberated and allowed to enter society at large. So great was the fear of assimilation and intermarriage that it found echo even in the writings of so different a character as Morris Joseph a hundred years later, who was a Reform minister in England and whose congregants had long been used to peace and prosperity. For him 'Every Jew who contemplates marriage outside the pale must regard himself as paving the way to a disruption which will be the final, as it will be the culminating disaster in the history of our people.'[18]

The novelist Israel Zangwill reflected the changing attitudes within Anglo-Jewry in his book *Children of the Ghetto* which followed the lives of those born in the dense Jewish settlement of the East End of London, but who did not necessarily remain there or maintain its Jewish mores:

◆ 'Why postpone the inevitable?' asked Sidney calmly ... 'It's all romantic fudge, the idea of perpetual isolation. You get into little cliques, and mistake narrow-mindedness for fidelity to an ideal. I can live for months and forget that there are such beings as Jews in the world.'

The table thrilled with horror, without, however, quite believing in the speaker's wickedness.

'A man and a wife of different religions can never know true happiness,' said the hostess.

'Granted,' retorted Sidney. 'But why shouldn't Jews without Judaism marry Christians without Christianity?'[19]

The process of emancipation not only brought an increased rate of Jews marrying non-Jews, as was feared, but also weakened internal communal authority and lessened the sanctions available to the leadership to combat it. Civil marriage had been introduced in England in 1837 and enabled mixed-faith couples to avoid having to choose between one religious establishment or the other and to have a non-denominational ceremony. Some Jewish parents tried to exert control over their children through financial means, disinheriting any that married out of the faith. One case that attracted much adverse public attention was that of Samuel Montagu, the first Lord Swaythling, who died in 1911. In his will he left his son, Edwin, the Liberal MP and later Secretary of State for India, a life interest in his estate which provided a large annual income. However, it was on condition that Edwin – then a bachelor and with little regard for his Jewish roots – always remained a Jew and did not marry out of the faith. When Edwin later wished to marry Venetia Stanley, daughter of the fourth Lord Sheffield, who was non-Jewish, the matter was resolved by her converting to Judaism. However, it was purely a sham conversion in order not to jeopardize the inheritance, and their only child was not brought up Jewish. Such cases had the unfortunate side effect of bringing into question the sincerity of much more genuine proselytes and of causing conversion to be regarded by some authorities as 'a backdoor to intermarriage'. The result was a marked unwillingness to accept converts from the mid

1930s, although this did little to stop intermarriage itself.

By 1945 the intermarriage figures so alarmed the Orthodox rabbinate in Britain that it passed an edict barring those who had married out of the faith from becoming members of a synagogue and declaring that those who were members already should not be allowed to hold any office within the congregation. The failure of such measures to have any impact on the still spiralling rate led to comparisons with the devastation caused by the Holocaust. In 1971 the then Chief Rabbi, Immanuel Jakobovits, used language that was highly emotional but very typical of prevailing rabbinic attitudes:

◆ That this process of attrition is infinitely less dramatic than the mass-slaughter of six million Jews only aggravates the situation. When Jews are lost through register-office marriages instead of gas chambers, no one weeps, protests or demonstrates … The worst cancer is the painless type; unaware of the danger signals, the patient will not even resort to a doctor until it is too late. Intermarriage is such a scourge.[20]

It became commonplace for preachers to accuse Jews who married non-Jews of continuing Hitler's work for him or adding 'another nail in the coffin of Judaism'. A series of adverts in the late 1980s in the widely-read weekly paper, *The Jewish Chronicle*, openly used guilt as a weapon by warning those considering intermarriage that 'Millions of heroic Jewish Martyrs have given their very lives in order that you and your children should remain Jewish. Dare you insult their eternal memory by marrying out of the faith?'[21] The other main tactic was to try to reverse the high level of integration which led to mixed-faith marriages, partly through intensifying Jewish education – by establishing Jewish day schools and improving adult education – and partly through discouraging social intercourse between Jews and non-Jews in the first place. A favourite illustration often recounted by rabbis was the trite but revealing anecdote of a Jew standing at a bus stop who was asked the time by a young man in the queue. He refused to answer even though he was wearing a watch. When asked why he was being so unhelpful, he replied, 'If I tell you the time, you will thank me and we will start chatting. When the bus comes, you will sit next to me. As we converse, you will learn where I live and one day you may drop in to look me up. You will see I have a beautiful daughter, fall in love with her and ask her hand in marriage – and I don't want a son-in-law who has not even got a watch!' Behind the surface humour was a deadly serious message: it is too late to argue with your children when they bring home a non-Jewish partner. The only solution is to stop them meeting in the first place. The best antidote to marrying out is only 'mixing in'.

A very different stance was taken by the Reform Synagogues of Great Britain. They were no more in favour than the Orthodox, but recognized that mixed-faith marriages were a reality of modern life. Rabbi Dow Marmur summed up the dilemma facing any exponent of integrated living:

◆ How will our children look upon us if we, on the one hand, encourage them to go to the best schools and universities, join the ranks of the professions and mix in the world of business and industry but, on the other, attempt to isolate them socially from the very environment to which they wish to belong?[22]

To put it another way, undergraduates who study together in the lecture halls may later fall in love in the student lounge. It was also appreciated that condemnation not only failed to stem this trend, but just resulted in alienating the couple from the Jewish community. Reform synagogues therefore adopted a new policy of encouraging the Jewish partners to maintain contact with the community and welcoming their non-Jewish spouses, and their children, if they too wished to participate in religious, social or educational activities. In 1989 the first of a pioneering series of seminars in London and the provinces took place at the Sternberg Centre entitled 'I'm Jewish, My Partner Isn't' whose object was to help mixed-faith couples discuss the issues facing them sympathetically and examine the options constructively. There was no attempt to split the relationship or convert the non-Jewish partner. The seminars met with harsh criticism from those opposed to such openness, with accusations that it was giving a green light to assimilation and condoning the unthinkable. However, the hundreds of couples of all ages who attended the seminars – some engaged, some recently wed, some married for twenty years or more – indicated that they answered a need that was sorely felt. 'At last I can come out of the closet' said many a participant, while Jeremy's sentiments were expressed time and time again by countless others: 'I felt so isolated before – it's good to know that there are others like me, and great to speak to people in the same situation as myself.' Despite being part of a sizable statistic, many of those in mixed-faith relationships felt they were without any support or point of reference.

In a curious way, the seminars also proved an important development for the rabbis themselves. Many of them had felt torn by a dual loyalty: they wished to preserve Jewish tradition and felt obliged to condemn outmarriage in general because of its potential threat to the survival of the community; yet they also wanted to be helpful on an individual basis to members of their congregation who were in a mixed-faith relationship. As one rabbi put it: 'When a person I know and respect says, "Look, I'm in love and it's the best thing that has ever happened to me", who am I to tell him he is wrong?' For such rabbis there was the difficult tightrope to walk of opposing outmarriage, but not those involved. The result was often condemnation from both sides – for not being severe enough and for not being accommodating enough – although the seminars themselves remained popular. They also had the effect of helping to remove the taboo from the subject of mixed-faith marriages and changing it from a topic fit only for abuse to a matter of serious discussion. It became placed high on the communal agenda of British Jewry.

The Liberal Synagogues, a smaller and more radical group, had long taken the attitude that the traditional definition of Jewish status – having a Jewish mother – was illogical: having a Jewish mother gave no guarantee a child would be brought up Jewish. It was also considered unfair on those children of a non-Jewish mother and a Jewish father who did receive a strong Jewish identity. In the early decades of the twentieth century, therefore, the Liberals accepted as Jewish anyone who had one Jewish parent (irrespective of their gender) and who received a Jewish education and home life. Although this position put the Liberals at odds with the rest of British Jewry, it did prove a welcome development for Jewish men with non-Jewish wives who wanted their children to be Jewish.

The number of Jews with Christian partners was so great that they were a well-recognized phenomenon in the general community too and became a much-used stereotype in the entertainment media. It was used in the very first talking film *The Jazz Singer* in 1927, mirroring the burgeoning clash between Jewish ethnic identity and the appeal of wider society. However, it was in the 1970s and 1980s, by which time mixed-faith marriages had become widespread, that there was a plethora of films featuring Jews in relationships with non-Jews: *The Heartbreak Kid, Portnoy's Complaint, Dirty Dancing, The Way We Were, When Harry Met Sally*. Woody Allen virtually specialized in the subject, with memorable portrayals such as *Annie Hall* and *Manhattan*. Jewish-Christian marriages were considered sufficiently commonplace and uncontroversial to occur in 'family viewing' television and to be the source of both comedy and drama series such as *Bridget Loves Bernie* and *Thirtysomething*. The next step was reached in 1995, when Hollywood – always anxious not to outrage public opinion – produced *Corrina, Corrina*, concerning a white Jew who falls in love with a black Christian. Its release was a barometer of social change, indicating that Jewish mixed-faith relationships were becoming mixed-race relationships as well.

Islam, like Judaism and Christianity, inherited much of the teachings of the Hebrew Bible. It, too, regarded marriage not only as a vehicle for physical and emotional love between men and women, but as a way of preserving the Islamic faith and transmitting it to the next generation. Muhammed is reported to have said 'When one is married, he secures half of his religion. So let him fear God in the other half.' A shared faith is considered a vital aspect of Islamic marriage and a Muslim is expected to marry a fellow-Muslim. Despite this ideal, however, certain exceptions are permitted. The Koran declares:

> Lawful unto you in marriage
> Are not only chaste women
> Who are believers, but
> Chaste women among
> The People of the Book.[23]

In effect, this means that a Muslim man can marry a Jewish or Christian woman. The marriage is considered valid, and the woman has the same rights and status as if she was a Muslim. The only restriction is that she will not inherit in the estate of her husband when he dies, as heirs have to be of the same religion as the deceased, although she can be given up to a third of the estate through a will. Her conversion is not necessary, although it is regarded as desirable. In many instances, communal pressure and family expectations mean that the woman has to convert if the couple do not wish to be ostracized. A Muslim woman, though, may not take a Jewish or Christian husband. Even if she is married according to state law, the marriage is null and void under Islamic law. The discrepancy between the sexes is because the religious status of the children follows the father, and so children of a Muslim mother and a non-Muslim father would be lost to the faith. Marriage between a Muslim male with a member of any faith other than Judaism or Christianity is strictly forbidden, unless the person converts to Islam. Some more liberal authorities have suggested extending the definition of 'People of the Book' to include other religious groups who have Holy Books, such as Sikhs and Hindus, but this is not generally accepted.

At present there are an estimated two to three million Muslims in Britain. Individual Muslims had been in the country for a considerable time, but the major migration occurred in the 1960s and 1970s. The relative newness of the community has meant that assimilation has not yet taken hold to the extent it has done with Jews, but already there have been major changes in the marriage patterns. For the majority of families, it was the accepted custom that parents had an important, if not decisive, role in selecting suitable marriage partners for their children. This became all the more important now that they were surrounded by a society that was part Christian, part secular and which often appeared at variance with traditional Islamic values. Yet parents and communal leaders found they faced a double problem.

One is that many of the second generation had already been influenced by Western values and resented being denied the freedom to choose their own partner. When they did succeed in establishing the right to make their own marital choice, the majority still married within their faith as they were still imbued with a strong ethnic and religious identity. Nevertheless, it signalled a lessening of parental and communal control, which is now being felt even more so with the children of those couples. They take it for granted that they too will marry 'for love' and, being more integrated in wider society than their parents, they are likely to find that love in non-Muslim partners. While the outmarriage rate is described as a trickle rather than a torrent, the religious leadership is aware that it may well increase rapidly in the next few decades. There are no exact figures available currently, but estimates suggest that around 500 Muslim women marry non-Muslim men each year. Those Muslim men who marry non-Muslim women largely marry Jews and Christians – which, as was seen above, are permissible unions. On the assumption that such households are Muslim ones, they are not counted as mixed-faith marriages. However, this assumption may be open to challenge as the third and much more secular generation of British Muslims grow up. They may be less willing – or less able – to insist that a Christian or Jewish wife adopts the Muslim way of life, and marriages to 'People of the Book' may in reality lead to households that are dual-faith or entirely secular. The high number of converts to Islam in Britain – some 10,000 in recent years, many converting because of marriage – has helped to delay this scenario, but the beginnings of it are already becoming apparent. As Ahmed, a highly articulate computer programmer, whose Muslim parents feel that he is losing touch with his roots, explained:

◆ If Jane [who considers herself Christian, but is not active in the Church] is willing to accept me as I am without making me change my lifestyle or beliefs, how can I reasonably demand that she changes hers? Anyway, I am not sure if I want her to. It would only be for my parents' sake and it would be desperately unfair to impose it on her just to please them. I would object if it was the other way round. Thankfully, in today's society there's a very large middle ground – that's how we met, and that's where we intend to stay.

The other problem was that many of those from India and Pakistan had observed a version of the Hindu caste system and had only married within certain groups or families. They therefore brought over for their children a marriage partner from their country of origin, who was from what was considered to be the right circle or who was a distant cousin. In cases where the newly-arrived groom had no command of English and had an inferior education to his British-educated bride, consider-able tensions arose. Several marriages broke down completely and there was a rise in the divorce rate from 'overseas marriages'. The crisis coincided with a tightening of British immigration laws, which restricted the traffic in importing husbands and wives from abroad. The combination of both factors led many families to realign their priorities. It was no longer considered so necessary to marry within the traditional circles, and instead it was sufficient to marry a fellow-Muslim whatever his or her background. This 'democratization' process has resulted in British-born Muslims finding mates among other British-born Muslims. This means they are often more compatible in terms of lifestyle and education, but it is hastening the rate of assimilation, because the influence of traditional Islam has been stemmed now that the flow from abroad has dried up. Here, too, the community is facing a chal-lenge which it feels may lead to a breakdown of its current structure and a likelihood of mixed-faith marriages in the next generation.

The three 'Abrahamic faiths' – Judaism, Christianity, Islam – which account for the religious background of the vast majority of those in Britain, all possess sacred Scriptures which are opposed to mixed-faith marriages. The other main reli-gions represented in Britain today have a more open attitude in theory, even if practice dictates otherwise. There is no specific prohibition of mixed-faith marriage in the Sikh holy book, the *Guru Granth Sahib*. However, it does contain a clear prefer-ence for shared beliefs: 'They are not man and wife who have physical contact only. Only they are truly wedded who have one spirit in two bodies.'[24] In *Prem Sumarag*, a book on Sikh code of conduct, it is laid down that fathers who select a husband for their daughters should choose a Sikh believer. In fact, the Sikh wedding ceremony itself begins with the officiant asking the bride and groom if they are both Sikhs and involves the couple walking round the *Guru Granth Sahib* four times.

At the same time, Sikhism admits that there are many paths to God and in principle there is nothing ungodly if a Sikh marries a non-Sikh. It is not so much a religious sin, but a cultural upset. The reason may differ from the theological objections seen in other faiths, but the effect can be just as problematic. Many Sikh families in Britain whose children marry out of the faith express dismay at what they regard as a threat to family traditions. Karnel's parents reacted in this way:

◆ They could not give me a single religious reason why I should not marry Barbara, who is from a Methodist tradition and highly principled, but they just keep on telling me it was a disgrace and the worst thing that had happened to the family in living memory.

For this reason, it is much preferred that if the marriage is definitely going ahead, the prospective partner becomes a Sikh. This applies whatever the religious background of the other person, although it is recognized that marriage with a Hindu can produce less strains, because of the various affinities between the two faiths. In many respects, therefore, the over-riding concern for Sikh parents is the compatibility of the couple and the relationship between the two families involved, rather than questions of salvation or purity of faith. At present it seems that the younger generation understands and respects these concerns – though does not always share them and will not impose them on their children. The result is that until now family loyalty and reluctant obedience has taken precedence over personal desires and has produced a relatively low outmarriage rate. However, there is a distinct sense of 'a lull before the storm' and greater conflict and increased inter-faith marriage is anticipated within the community.

In Hinduism, there is a curious blend of both permissive and restrictive attitudes. As is well known, Hindus traditionally marry within the caste system, in which the four main classes – priests, warriors, agriculturists and traders or servants – have been divided into hundreds of sub-castes. Each one represents a group that largely enjoys the same descent, follows the same profession, and observes the same family customs. They are the sole marriage pool from which a person can choose a partner, and marrying out of the caste can lead to being ostracized or, in more volatile circumstances, subject to attack. However, in Britain the practice of caste-marriages has received a strong challenge. This is partly because of the impact of British culture, whose liberal underpinning rejects what it regards as a discriminatory system. This has influenced younger Hindus, born and educated in this country, and led many to question the relevance of the caste system. Moreover, the relatively few number of Hindus in the country – some 800,000 – means that the availability of suitable marriage partners is limited and has led to broadening the range of choice beyond the immediate sub-caste. The gulf between the generations was highlighted by research at the beginning of the 1990s which indicated that nearly 50% of young Hindus expected a less traditional arrangement of their marriage than their parents expected to allow them.[25] Vanmali, a 19-year-old Hindu raised in Coventry, is adamant about the path he will take:

◆ When I fall in love, it will be because of the person, not because of her ancestors and what they did or didn't do hundreds of years ago in India. Of course, I don't want to upset my parents needlessly, but if they're realistic they should be only too delighted if I marry another Hindu, forget about what caste she is. I am sure some of my friends will marry non-Hindus, not deliberately, but because that is who they mix with.

Despite the strict regulations concerning internal caste-marriages, mixed-faith relationships are not banned in the Hindu Scriptures, the Vedas. This may be simply because such a situation was not envisaged at the time. Nevertheless, contact with other religions and the influence they may have are not seen as threatening. In some areas, caste was regarded as almost more important than faith. Thus it is, and always has been, normal for Punjabis from Hindu and Sikh families to intermarry if the caste was the same. A similar pattern occurs between Hindus and Jains in Gujarat. Indeed, the elasticity of Hindu theology allows a Hindu to adopt the non-Hindu beliefs and practices of his/her partner without ceasing to be a Hindu. Moreover, having a faith is regarded as much more important than the particular faith to which one adheres. Providing the local priest agrees, a full Hindu wedding ceremony can be performed in a temple for a Hindu marrying a person of another faith. The religious status of children often follows that of the father, but this is not a strict rule. Much depends on the upbringing children receive, and Hinduism prefers to accept a person's self-identity as the guiding factor rather than legal definitions to which they have to conform. It should be noted, though, that there is a difference between the teachings of the faith and the feelings of parents. Hindu families in Britain, for instance, may be tolerant of other faiths but still wish their children to marry a fellow Hindu and share the same cultural background. When someone does marry out of the faith, it can lead to tension and recriminations. This is particularly the case if the other partner is a Muslim – not so much because of religious objections, but because of the political and historical clashes between the two faiths. There is also a certain resentment against what Professor Robert Jackson calls 'the feeling of one-way traffic': that Hindu girls have to become Muslim to marry a Muslim, while Muslim girls are forbidden from marrying Hindus. Hindu authorities have no figures for members of the community who choose non-Hindu partners. The common view is that the numbers are small at present, but will increase sharply in the future for two reasons: social integration at school and in the workplace will lead to mixed-faith relationships; cultural integration will lessen the attachment of Hindus to their tradition and the desire to continue it.

Buddhism is the religion for which mixed-faith marriages present the least problems of all. Its sacred texts have nothing to say on the subject, nor is it mentioned in later teachings. The main thrust of Buddhism is the attainment of personal enlightenment, with each individual engaged on their own spiritual journey. Teachings of truth can be accepted from whatever source they come and there is no sense of exclusivity. Buddhism allows its adherents to have more than one religious allegiance, and so marriage with a person of another faith poses no difficulty. Moreover, the fact that celibacy, not marriage, is the highest ideal, is indicative of the Buddhist emphasis on personal fulfilment rather than with handing down the faith to future generations. Mixed-faith marriages are therefore not seen as either betraying family traditions or clouding the true faith. Buddhists may be married in the manner and place of worship of any other religion, such as in church. There is no Buddhist wedding service – the marriage is conducted through the procedures of the civil authorities – but a Buddhist and non-Buddhist who wish to receive the blessing by a monk that follows the civil ceremony may do so. In certain circumstances a monk might counsel a Buddhist not to proceed with a proposed marriage to a member of another faith: for instance, if it was to a Muslim who felt that Buddhist practices were distasteful and who objected to the presence of a Buddha in the home, regarding it as an idol. In these cases, though, the objection would be purely on the practical grounds of possible disharmony rather than over religious principles. In keeping with its stress on the individual, there is no concern over which particular faith the children pursue. Buddhists parents may well pass on Buddhist teachings, but ultimately the children have to seek their own enlightenment in whichever way is most appropriate for them. The commitment a couple make in marriage is to maintain a bond with each other, and does not involve ensuring the continuity of the faith through children. There is no sense of failure or any conflict if the children choose another path. Put simply, for Buddhists the whole matter of mixed-faith marriages is a non-issue.

Buddhism has relatively few members in Britain compared to the other major religions, but its attitude to mixed-faith marriages may prove to be the most influential. Christians, Hindus, Jews, Muslims and Sikhs who fall in love with each other may have enormous respect for the views of their family and the stipulations of their faith, but many find that personal emotions take precedence over religious traditions. In former years the reverse would have been true. The key question is why this revolution has taken place.

Notes

1 Genesis 24:3–4
2 Genesis 26:34–5; Genesis 27:46; Genesis 28:1
3 Exodus 34:15–16
4 Deuteronomy 7:1–4
5 Exodus 2:21; Judges 14:1; Malachi 2:11
6 Leviticus 24:10–11; Numbers 25:6-15; see also 1 Kings 11:1–13
7 Ezra 9:10–14; 10:1–11; Nehemiah 13:23–30
8 1 Corinthians 7:12–16
9 2 Corinthians 6:14–15
10 Ephesians 5:21–31
11 quoted in Heron, Alasdair, *Two Churches, One Love,* Dublin, APCK, 1977, p. xiv
12 Shakespeare, William, *Othello*, Act 1, Scene 1, 88–9 and 112–13
13 Kindregan, Charles P., *A Theology of Marriage*, Milwaukee, Bruce Publishing Company, 1967, pp.131–2
14 *Mixed Marriages – The Revised Directory Promulgated by the Bishops' Conference of England and Wales*, London, Catholic Truth Society, 1990, p. 19
15 For further details see *The Marriage of Adherents of Other Faiths in Anglican Churches*, General Synod of the Church of England, Board of Mission Occasional Paper No.1 (1992); *Guidelines for the Celebration of Mixed-faith Marriages in Church*, General Synod of the Church of England, Board of Mission Occasional Paper No.2 (1992) from where material has been taken

16 *Liberation*, Paris, 5 November 1986
17 Babylonian Talmud, Avodah Zarah 36b, Yevamot 45a
18 Joseph, Morris, *Judaism as Creed and Life*, London, Routledge and Kegan Paul, 1903, p.186
19 Zangwill, Israel, *Children of the Ghetto*, 1st published 1892; London, White Lion, 1972 p. 249
20 Jakobovits, Immanuel, *Intermarriage and Conversion*, London, United Synagogue, 1971, p. 4
21 *The Guardian*, London, 26 July 1994; *The Jewish Chronicle*, London, 11 December 1987
22 Marmur, Dow, *Intermarriage*, London, Reform Synagogues of Great Britain, 1973, p. 15
23 Sura 5, verse 6
24 quoted in Cole and Sambhi, *The Sikhs: Their Religious Beliefs and Practices*, London, Routledge and Kegan Paul, 1978, p. 116
25 Stopes-Roe, M. and Cochrane, R., *Citizens of This Country: The Asian-British*, London, Multilingual Matters, 1990, p. 36

Chapter Three

We have reason to fall in love

The five factors that lead to mixed-faith relationships
and the influences that affect individual lives

For Pam, the reason behind her Christian-Muslim marriage is simple and straightforward: 'All I can tell you is that I fell in love with Rashid because I fell in love with him. What more is there to say?' Perhaps in her case that is the full story, but for many other mixed-faith couples there is a vast range of factors that have led them to cross the religious frontiers, often braving the disapproval of others, and sometimes reversing their own stated intentions. There is no blanket pattern; different reasons, and different combinations of them, will apply to each individual. They may not even be fully aware of them at the time of their marriage. Many have no difficulty answering the rhetorical accusation often flung at them by parents – 'I hope you know what you're doing to us' – but they might need more time in articulating a response to the question 'Why couldn't you choose someone from the same faith?' The twenty or more reasons that might form a reply can be grouped into five overall headings: changes within wider society, developments within the religious communities, dynamics within the family, personal factors and chance.

The changes within wider society are certainly the most crucial reason for the growth in mixed-faith marriages, although they are still only part of the answer. Mention has already been made of the transformation of society from one that was strictly divided into groups and which judged people by the category to which they belonged, to one that valued the principles of egalitarianism and treated people as individuals. Some prejudices against those who were 'different' may have survived intact, but educational opportunities, access to jobs, entry into the higher echelons of political and civic institutions, and new residential patterns, meant that faith groups began to leave both their physical and mental ghettos and mingle with each other to an extent that had never happened before. Patrick was no longer a Catholic, David was no longer a Jew, but both were Englishmen; moreover, both were students in the chemistry department at university, alongside women who shared the same interest. 'What do you do?' superseded 'What religion do you belong to?' as the key question when meeting someone new, particularly of the opposite sex. In the past, it was scattered individuals who broke away from the mores of their religious groups to form unions with each other. Now it was the groups themselves that were coming much closer: the majority faith and culture – the Church of England – was extending a welcome to all the other components in society and including them in its daily affairs. At the same time the minority groups – Catholics, Jews and later Muslims, Hindus and others – leapt at the opportunity to achieve this integration. Indeed, much of their effort in previous years had been spent trying to gain political and social emancipation, either through the statute books or by making inroads into the cultural life of the country. Once this 'macro relationship' occurred, it was inevitable that a host of 'micro relationships' would follow, with members of the different constituent groups establishing close bonds with each other in the increasingly diverse mixture of British society. As Rabbi Alexander Schindler put it pithily, 'We live in an open society, and intermarriage is the sting which comes to us in the honey of our freedom.'

An important element is not just the legislative reforms which brought the more open society into being, but the change in popular mood which predated them and paved their way. The rise of tolerance led to a decline in the sense of public disgrace that had helped prevent many would-be mixed-faith marriages occurring. Hetty, now in her seventies, well remembers the non-Jewish boyfriend she loved and lost in her youth because both sets of parents refused to allow the match to proceed. 'It simply wasn't the done thing. It is hard to say who was more appalled – his father or my father – but they were both agreed that it had to stop.' Her own experience did not stop her expressing concern when her grandson got his way and married out of the faith, although she admits that part of her felt very envious at the freedom he has that she did not. 'Everything has changed now – and mixed-marriage hardly seems to matter. It was so different in my day.' The outrage that greeted such unions barely fifty years ago has now been replaced by indifference on the part of society and by a weary acceptance from most parents. They may have reservations in their hearts, but most feel that the thrust of social patterns today makes their objections untenable and leaves them with little option but to shrug their shoulders. The transition of society from an age of personal endeavour based on moral qualities to an age of technology dependent on scientific skills has resulted in religious issues departing from the stage of public life and being a matter of private scruples only. Moreover, the religious pluralism that now exists in Britain – with many a church occupying the same road as a mosque or synagogue – has helped make faith appear in the eyes of many to lack objective truth and be a subjective matter; in effect, religious viewpoints have lost much of their role as a criterion for public judgments. If an individual conforms to them or deviates from them – be it a Catholic who has an abortion or a

Muslim who enjoys a pint of beer or a Sikh who cuts his hair – it is of no concern to society at large and does not affect that person's standing in it. Added to this is the effect of the liberal approach to social issues that has been adopted in the vast majority of schools over the last thirty years. It means that a whole generation of children have been taught, rightly, to avoid the prejudices of the past and be conscious of the common humanity of all people. One result of this is that they may then feel that parental objection to a partner of a different faith is simply racism and is to be dismissed as unacceptable.

At the same time, the concept of marriage has also undergone a radical change. For many, it is no longer a vehicle for transmitting family property rights, nor a means of perpetuating religious traditions. It is also no longer the union of two families, whilst its arrangement is not the prerogative of family heads, with the actual bride and groom being incidental players. Instead it is a personal matter for the couple concerned, with the family being the bystanders. Compatibility is not only judged by the two partners, but is seen as being dependent on their feelings for each other. Love is the determining factor. When Rashid told his father 'I am in love with someone non-Muslim' it was the first half of that sentence that was important to him, not the second half. When making a decision about their future together, his emotions took precedence over his background and convinced him that the marriage should go ahead. 'It's Pam that counts,' he said, 'not her religion.' This new attitude to marriage coincides with the unprecedented cult of the individual that has been the hallmark of recent years. In this framework, it matters not what the status is of one's partner – their class, colour, faith – but what they mean to the person concerned. Talk of 'marrying in' or 'marrying out' is as irrelevant to them as thermal underwear is to Aborigines.

Some individuals caught up in this new world found themselves unprepared for its consequences and were taken by surprise emotionally. David Daiches was brought up as a strictly Orthodox Jew and the son of the leading rabbi in Scotland. When he read English at Edinburgh University he felt torn between his religious roots and his social milieu:

◆ Deceit was forced on me by degrees. My father knew that girls attended the university lectures. Presumably it was all right if I got into conversation with a girl after a lecture … Was it all right to walk a few steps while talking to her? If so, how many? The position was ludicrous.

No one had warned me of the possibility that I might find some non-Jews more **sympathique** than any Jews I knew. This was a most disturbing revelation to me, and it made toeing the invisible line imposed by the policy of Jewish self-segregation not only physically almost impossible but a great strain psychologically … Thus it was that a policy of anguished reconsideration of the relation between my Jewish background and my non-Jewish environment was forced on me. It was a long and painful process … I had the sense of living on the edge of a precipice … of living in two worlds and sometimes in an abyss between them.[1]

For Daiches and others like him the struggle between the two conflicting realities in his life took place in early adulthood. For many others the meeting of cultures occurred at a much younger age, when they attended the local primary school. There they drew Christmas cards, sang Jewish folk songs, celebrated Diwali and learnt about Ramadan. The result was twofold: first, these cultural exchanges meant that ignorance, along with the suspicions and self-distancing that usually accompanied it, were swept away and replaced by mutual appreciation and understanding. In turn this made the old antagonisms between the faiths less likely and made personal intercourse more likely. Second, social access to those of a different faith was immediate and commonplace, with direct and predictable consequences. Primary school friendships led to secondary school relationships and continued afterwards either to living together or to being wed. Put bluntly, inter-dating ends in inter-marriage, and the roots lie as much in the nursery as they do in the college hall.

The social interchange between the faiths is not limited to schools, but happens in a wide range of avenues: sports, political groups, cultural activities, social clubs, special interest societies. The result is that those who meet there find that what they have in common is often of much greater importance – at least at that stage in their lives – than what divides them. As Pete (lapsed Church of Scotland) said about his Jewish fiancée: 'All I knew about Linda was that she was a brilliant chess-player. When we talked it was about chess or the people we knew. It never occurred to me to ask if she prayed and who to. It was months before I found out she was Jewish.' The work-place is another major source of mating, and although members of different faiths have long co-existed side by side, the changes in the social climate have meant that relationships have developed beyond the merely colleagual. The stereotype of the Jewish doctor who marries a Christian nurse represents not just the opportunities presented by the medical profession, but stands for men and women of all occupations who find that daily contact and common purpose create a bond that they wish to maintain for the rest of their lives. In fact the points of contact very often go much deeper than hobbies, but stem from the very similar upbringing individuals from different faiths can have. If their parents occupy the same socio-economic bracket and have similar standards of behaviour, their offspring can find that their journey through childhood and the teenage years has followed an almost identical path despite the religious differences. 'Our homes were both loving, middle-class, relatively prosperous, with a lot of importance attached to the arts, but also a strong concern for social issues,' said Clive 'and the fact that one of them was Christian and the other Hindu was almost an extra detail that got lost in the general mix.' His wife nodded vehemently and added 'Yes, of course we were aware of that distinction – but it was the shared sense of values and goals that was what drew us together.'

The tolerant attitude society has evinced to minority groups, including religious minorities, has led to members of those groups feeling more at ease in their relations with the majority culture and less inclined to live only in parts of the country in which they are surrounded by members of the same faith-community. Whereas being in a Jewish, Catholic or Hindu environment may have been important considerations in the past, now those individuals are also guided by good schools, clean air, larger gardens and other concerns which mean they will settle in areas that lack a sizable number of co-religionists. This in turn lessens their attachment to their traditional way of life and speeds up the process of assimilation. This has been evident in the most integrated of the minority religious groups, the Jewish community. The proportion of Jews living in intensely Jewish areas – originally the East End of London, now northwest London – has gradually dropped as a growing number of families move further afield into the Home Counties. They are no longer within walking distance of a synagogue, as before, and often not even in convenient driving distance. The result is that occasional forays are made for major festivals, but in reality they are divorced from the Jewish community and daily life for them and their children becomes increasingly assimilated. Several years later, when those parents are confronted by their offspring announcing their engagement to a non-Jewish partner, they may feel a sense of regret but in the cold light of their own decisions they cannot be surprised.

The geographical dispersion within Britain is part of a larger worldwide trend involving the movement of millions of people from the place of origin – often where they were part of a religious majority – to new areas of settlement. In some cases, this has been a voluntary movement by those seeking higher standards of living or better educational opportunities for their children, such as Hindus and Sikhs who were eligible for British citizenship and arrived in the decades following Indian Independence in 1947. In other cases, it has been the result of enforced flight from direct persecution or political upheavals. This has ranged from Jews fleeing Russia in the 1880s and Central Europe in the 1930s to Muslims expelled from Uganda in 1972. Britain in particular has attracted many immigrants partly because of its high living standard, partly because of its links with former colonies and with the Commonwealth, and partly because of its, till recently, liberal laws on asylum and immigration. The migration of individuals and large groups has been facilitated in the latter half of the twentieth century by ever-quicker and easier methods of international transport.

Another reason for the geographical dispersion is the job market. At times of high unemployment, many families have found it necessary to move to a new area in order to secure employment. Enforced mobility has also applied in better times owing to the growth of large multinational corporations who often expect their employees to move around the country; failure to do so can result in forfeiting any chances of promotion or losing one's position entirely. Once again, the effect is to cut individuals off from their own communities, while there is even greater impact on young children, who grow up far from the religious ecology in which their parents were raised. A study of working adults in the State of Iowa in the mid-1950s bears witness to this: whereas the rate of mixed-faith families was 27.2% amongst blue-collar workers, it was 46.8% amongst white-collar workers.

It is open to debate whether the actual standard of living of individuals may have some bearing on their marriage pattern. One suggestion is that those with lower income are more likely to intermarry. This would be because newer minority faiths often have no central funding, long-held endowments, or buildings of worship that have been handed down the ages. All costs have to be borne by their members, and those members who cannot pay synagogue membership fees or purchase of *halal* meat may opt out of communal life and mix in wider circles. It may also be that those on lower incomes prefer to travel less far afield to work and, for instance, will both work at and live close by the local factory and will therefore fraternize more with fellow workers and their families, despite the different religious and cultural backgrounds. This also applies to immigrants from abroad who have a low economic status and who are forced to settle in areas of cheap rent, where they mix with indigenous workers also at the bottom of the economic ladder. Whilst their different faiths may at first cause some reserve on the part of the immigrants and resentment on the part of the existing community, their common struggle and daily routine often bridges the initial divide and leads to cross-relationships. Of course, sometimes the gulf proves irreconcilable, particularly when religious differences are compounded by political strife, as in Northern Ireland. Marriages between Protestants and Catholics tend to be more unacceptable in working-class circles there. Instead, it is amongst the middle classes that such unions are more common, partly because a higher level of education can lead to more tolerance and partly because they are more able to move to a non-sectarian area where they will feel more at ease.[2]

Mixed-faith marriages can also be a way of moving up the economic and social ladder. Those who are considered outsiders for racial and religious reasons can overcome their isolation by marrying into those who are part of the establishment or, if not that high, are at least 'accepted'. Ron – a Hindu who is a surveyor by profession – married Kaye for love, but recognizes that if they had not met he would almost certainly have married another white Church of England girl:

◆ Now that I am living in England, I want to be part of the country and lay down roots. Marrying a Christian is part of that and it means my children won't be on the edge of things in the way that

I was as a child. Kaye is a wonderful wife and I would not want anyone else. I saw all sorts of qualities in her when we met. Being properly English was one of them. I might have an English passport, but it's just a piece of paper; she has it in her blood.

There are many, by contrast, who feel that emotional security can best be achieved through marrying within one's own group; but for those who seek social security in the majority culture, marriage is the fast-track route. Jews, too, have often sought social acceptance through ties of marriage. In the late nineteenth century it became fashionable for wealthy Jewish families to seek a match within the aristocracy for their offspring. For their part, those already embedded in society found such unions offered benefits to them too – younger sons of the aristocracy did not usually inherit much of their father's estate and were left looking for means of support, while even the heirs often needed an influx of 'new money' if the family houses and grounds were to be preserved intact. It was an arrangement of mutual convenience, although not totally opportunistic, as the partners-to-be were moving in the same circles, and perhaps even friendly with each other's brother or sister. There are advantages also to the Kayes of modern times. For them, a second-generation Hindu husband can offer the respect for womanhood and appreciation of motherhood that English husbands might regard as quaint and old-fashioned. As she herself remarked: 'When we were courting it was so different. I can't quite explain how, but I know he treated me differently from the way all my previous boyfriends had.' For them and many other mixed-faith couples there can be solid practical benefits, whether they are consciously aware of them or not.

Another change in society that has increased the rate of mixed-faith marriages has been the emancipation of women. In previous centuries and up to the middle of the twentieth century, it was predominantly the men who married out of the faith for three reasons: first, because they took the initiative in proposing marriage and were in the position of initiating rather than responding; second, because sons had greater freedom than daughters in decision-making within the family, and could therefore carve a new path despite parental opposition; third, because they had greater mobility through their jobs and were more likely to move to, or work in, areas inhabited by members of other faith-groups. The enormous advances for women in terms of their access to higher levels of education and rights of employment have given women an autonomy and mobility that they lacked before. They are more likely to want to live away from their parents on achieving adulthood, while their financial independence makes this possible. Even before they start employment, many have experienced three years residence in a different part of the country whilst at college. The result is that in the more integrated faith-groups, the rate of females marrying out of their community has grown rapidly and is almost as high as the male rate. Pilot studies in Britain amongst the Jewish community in the 1990s, for instance, show that 47% of those contracting marriages with non-Jews are females. Another aspect of Jewish females is that a high proportion of them attend university and are not only exposed to greater contact with non-Jews, but are sometimes seen as 'high achievers' and, therefore, as attractive marriage partners. It is true that in some ways Jewish females who marry out cause less problems in terms of the internal status of children – which follows that of the mother – but in the past Jewish women have not married out as much as did the menfolk for the three reasons already cited. More recent immigrant faiths, whose women have so far integrated less than the men, show a lower rate: with only 16% of Muslims and 35% of Hindus marrying out being women. The large discrepancy between the two figures may be because the status of children in Muslim families follows that of the father, and so there is more pressure against Muslim women marrying out of their religion. However, as the second- and third-generation Muslim and Hindu women become part of British society more and take advantage of the social and economic opportunities, it is anticipated that they too will marry out of their faith as much as their male counterparts.

The changes in society may be crucial, but equally important are developments within the religious communities themselves. The changes in society only become relevant when they are matched by a response from within the religious groups, and particularly when those groups lose the desire for cohesion or when their commitment to the future weakens. The collapse in the religious identity of many households has been a key factor in this process. In many ways Jenny's story is typical and speaks for a whole generation who feel that they have been religiously orphaned and given no clear sense of direction, or even roots to cling on to:

◆ I know I am Church of England – because that's what it says on my baptism certificate, which I got when I was a few weeks old. But as I was never taken to church or Sunday school after that, I feel it doesn't really mean much. It's like saying I am a Lancashire girl because I was born in Bolton – okay, it's true, but so what? Anyway, I am not an atheist – because I do believe in a God – but I don't really know in what way or how to express it in a religious sense. I suppose it means being moral – and that's fine; but I don't have any real understanding of rituals or festivals to give it a religious setting. And I suppose that would not have bothered me too much – a shame, but not a problem – unless there had been all that fuss over Len being Jewish and not wanting to get married in church. Suddenly my family was up in arms – I would be the first one not to have a church ceremony. I was stunned at first. Then I got furious. How dare they expect me to keep up a tradition they'd never bothered to pass on? If they had given me absolutely no reason for marrying in, why shouldn't I marry out?

For his part, Len provided a mirror image, coming from a family that was more Jewish in name than in deed:

◆ It was a fairly typical story. We observed the High Holy Days every year, but did precious little in between. I was Jewish once a year! True, my mother wouldn't have pork in the house, but there was no objection to eating it in restaurants or at friends' homes. That struck me as having double standards, but what was worse was the whole business of driving to synagogue when it is supposed to be forbidden [at festivals and sabbaths] and then parking round the corner and pretending we had walked there. I remember feeling that was awful – especially when the point of going to services was to pray to God and be open and sincere, and I was determined that when I grew up I would either do it properly or not at all. With hindsight I guess it was inevitable that with that sort of background it was bound to be not at all. Meeting Jenny didn't really drag me away from my Judaism because it was never really there in the first place. And it wasn't just my family. Most of my friends came from similar situations. What surprises me now is not that so many have married non-Jews like I have, but that some have still married Jews. It certainly wasn't for religious reasons.

The lack of religious identity can be such that in many cases the subject of religion is never raised until the relationship is well established, and the couple are not even aware that there is a religious difference between them. When Ned said of his fiancée 'I didn't realize she was Jewish until we'd been going out for eight months, and then it came up for some reason', it was not because they were uncommunicative, but simply because their religious background was such a non-issue for them that it never warranted a mention.

If there is no doubt that religiously-lapsed homes encourage mixed-faith marriages – or at least don't discourage them – there is an intriguing uncertainty as to the impact of high or low levels of religious education. The conventional view is that children who have little tuition in their faith – whether from Sunday schools or day schools – are bound to have less ties to that faith on the grounds that knowledge brings understanding, appreciation and commitment. They are therefore more prone to be tempted away from it, less bothered about passing it on to their children and more likely to be the ones who enter mixed-faith marriages. A series of surveys in the 1950s gave statistical backing to this notion. In Washington, for instance, the inter-marriage rate of Jewish married men who had attended a religion school as children was 16.4%, whereas for those who had not attended it was almost double at 30.2%. As Robert said, 'When I walk into a synagogue – which isn't very often – I haven't a clue what to do. I know you could say it's up to me to find out, but I was never taught as a child and frankly I don't really have the time or interest to find out now.' On being quizzed about his time and why he could not use leisure hours to read up about Judaism or attend classes, he added, 'At the end of the day, it's not that I don't have the time – if I wanted to, I could make time – it's more that I don't have the motivation.' Not surprisingly, Robert's girlfriends have nearly all been non-Jewish and there is every reason to suppose his wife will be too. Nicky, newly wed, voiced similar feelings from a different perspective:

◆ My parents were both Catholic and often told me I was Catholic but never gave me any education in the faith or sent me to Sunday school. In a sense what they gave me has remained – the label: I am still a Catholic but now I have a non-Catholic husband. I think it would be daft perpetuating the same meaningless tag to any children we have, quite apart from the fact that I wouldn't know what else to tell them; so I won't bring them up to consider them-selves Catholic, and I'll either leave the religious input to my husband or hope they pick something up from school.

As a result of such telling evidence, many of the minority faith-communities who have been alarmed at the rate of intermarriage amongst their members have made increased education a central strategy in their campaign to halt the trend. This has taken a dual form: first in providing extracurricular classes for children after school or at the weekends. Muslim children often attend special lessons several times a week, organized by communal leaders who rent rooms at local schools or youth centres. This used to be the pattern also in the Jewish community, although since the Second World War it has been increasingly relegated to just Sunday mornings owing to the pressure of schoolwork or the logistical difficulties presented by the children living far afield. To compensate for the extremely short amount of time this leaves for Jewish education – barely two hours a week – efforts have been made to improve its quality. Formal training in both Jewish knowledge and educational techniques is given to the teaching staff, who were previously often parents with goodwill and no grounding in either pedagogics or Jewish learning. At the same time advances have been made in improving educational materials, developing interesting textbooks and audiovisual equipment. The second approach has been to promote day school education with a religious character. Since the 1960s, the Jewish community has invested heavily in Jewish day school education at both primary and secondary levels. In recent years the Muslims have followed the same pattern, convinced that both the religious input and the same-faith milieu are the only ways to guarantee continuity of the faith. The network of Catholic schools around the country has been in existence for a considerable time and they have little difficulty in maintaining their rolls, with many parents accepting the oft-quoted Jesuit saying 'Give me a child till the age of seven and I will have him for the rest of his life'. Religious commitment and religious education are assumed to be closely related.

The thesis that religious day schools are the panacea to all problems, and in particular a solution to intermarriage, has been challenged in recent years. This has arisen from surveys among the Jewish community, but which may apply equally to others. The Brandeis study quoted above showed virtually no relationship between increased Jewish education and decreased intermarriage, other than those engaged in intensive Jewish learning from the ultra-Orthodox sector. The study, from a large target group spread over eight cities in 1992, revealed that for most Jews under 45, Jewish education appears to be no barrier to intermarriage. Exactly the same conclusion has come from pilot studies in Britain at the same time. Two thirds of Jews in mixed-faith marriages had attended religion school at least from the age of seven till the age of thirteen. Even more striking was that 20% had been at Jewish day schools. If these findings are repeated it either means that the Jewish studies departments at such schools need to be radically overhauled, or that the whole concept of using schools to combat outmarriage has to be reassessed. Muslim day schools are too new for their impact to be measured. The fact that they are currently battling with the government to gain state funding to open even more schools indicates they are convinced of their worth. However, the enormously high rate of Catholics entering mixed-faith marriages – some 70% – suggests that however much they know about their religion, it does not necessarily stop them choosing partners from other backgrounds. As a result of the above findings, it may be that no religious education increases the possibility of outmarriage, while a good religious education lessens it. However, it seems clear that the argument is over relative influence and not, as was originally supposed, a matter of absolute effect. Those who lack religious knowledge may still marry within the faith for other reasons – cultural bonds or family loyalty – while those who possess religious knowledge may still marry out of the faith for reasons outlined earlier. The critical question affecting those in the latter category – which will be examined later – is what relationship they maintain with the faith in which they are knowledgeable, but out of which they have married.

While the debate surrounding education simmers on, there is broad agreement over another factor affecting the internal life of the newer faith-communities: the loss of foreign-born grandparents. Generally, they were the least assimilated members of the family. Not only were they the ones most instilled with a strong religious identity, but those most capable of transmitting the religious heritage to their children and with an important role, too, for the grandchildren. Stephen, who comes from a Methodist family, echoed the experience of many from all faiths when he said, 'As a child, I knew exactly what God looked like – my grandfather.' He probably spoke for others too when he added, 'I'm pretty sure my grandchildren won't say the same about me. Somehow we've lost something very special when that generation passed away – call it a sense of awe, I can't say exactly – but I know they had it and we don't.'

The disappearance of this influence is part of the general pattern of diminishing religiosity of succeeding generations. Generally – but not always – the longer a Jewish, Muslim or Hindu family have been in Britain, the more integrated and less traditional they are. The first generation are immigrants, who often dress differently and may not even be familiar with English; they have no doubt where their main point of reference lies and, while appreciative of Britain's hospitality, regard their religious culture as their emotional homeland. The second generation are born in Britain and are heirs to conflict; they wish to be part of society but are heavily influenced by the home life which is often at variance with it; apart from their own inner conflict, they are also torn by the conflicting needs of their parents and children. For the third generation the emphasis has changed completely; they feel at home in wider society and regard it as their natural habitat; they still identify with their family traditions, although from afar, finding them quaint and somewhat disconcerting, and not necessarily a criterion for choosing a marriage partner. The advent of the fourth generation brings a decisive turning point: it is either the time of return for those who find that what society offers is insufficient spiritually and who now seek out their roots with an intensity that surprises their parents; or it is the final break with these roots by those who have no point of contact with them any more and for whom it is inconceivable that they have any bearing on how they conduct their lives. Thus there is a direct relationship between the number of generations members of a minority faith have been in the country and their level of mixed-faith marriage. The Washington study, quoted above, traced this pattern with stunning precision: it found that intermarriage increased from 1.4% in the foreign-born (the first generation), to 10.2% of the native-born to foreign parents (the second generation), to 17.9% of the native-born of native parents (the third generation).

A further, albeit much more minor, factor in the intermarriage pattern may be what could be termed a religious own-goal. The decades since the 1960s have been characterized by an explosion in inter-faith dialogue. Those who once fulminated over religious differences have now recognized not only that the real enemy is religious indifference, but also that it is a common enemy. Priests, rabbis and sheikhs now fear secularism much more than they fear each other. More positively, they have also come to appreciate common roots: how much they share ancient sources, how their quests have often intertwined and influenced each other, and how encountering different perspectives can not only bring new insights but reveal hidden aspects of one's own traditions. There is also a general consensus amongst many religious leaders – from the Pope to the Dalai Lama – that each faith contains truth and that there are many different paths to heaven. At a time of diminishing church and synagogue attendance, inter-faith dialogue has become a new growth industry. Many clerics have found to their surprise that on some levels they have more in common with a minister of a different faith than with a nominal member of their own faith, sharing a knowledge and enthusiasm that are often absent in the pews. As a result, inter-faith conferences have proved very attractive and have led to invitations to ministers of other religions to preach at, or speak in, churches and synagogues. The development of communication, respect and trust between the major religions is a wonderful advance, long overdue and capable of enriching both individual participants and society at large. However, it is possible that it can give a misleading impression to some: that the distinctions between the faiths are unimportant, and that they all carry the same message expressed in different ways. If this is the case, the argument goes, it matters not which faith one follows, so long as one has a faith. Sally lacks theological training but gives voice to a view held by many moderately-involved Christians:

◆ I think it's great that all the religious bigwigs are getting together. But it makes you think, doesn't it? I mean, what's important is being moral and God-fearing. That's what's at the root of it all, isn't it? So long as you keep to that, it doesn't matter what religion you are – or who you marry, if they also follow the same moral code.

… I've always tried to keep the Ten Commandments. My boyfriend is Muslim and he has even more! So I don't think I'm letting the Church down in any way. If anything, it's making me more aware of daily behaviour and dos and don'ts.

It is clear that Sally and others like her are not using inter-faith dialogue as an excuse to date and marry partners from a different faith, but it may be that it has created a climate of acceptability that has helped remove the stigma from mixed-faith relationships, so that when they happen there is less sense of private guilt or public outrage. Every time the Archbishop of Canterbury and the Chief Rabbi are photographed having tea together, it encourages a Jewish boy and a Christian girl to do the same. It would be a serious mistake if such dialogue were to cease because of this unintended side effect, but it would be equally foolish not to be aware of the climate it creates. The initial premise laid down in the inter-faith conference rooms of 'let us accept our religions on equal terms' inevitably changed to 'let us accept each other in mutual respect' and was heard by some in the streets as 'let us get together in mutual love'.

The result of all these various developments within the religious communities has been a decrease in religious will amongst many members of the faiths – less loyalty to past traditions, less intensity in their present observances, less commitment to future continuity. The anguished question posed in 1994 by the Chief Rabbi of Orthodox Jews to members of his flock – 'Will we have Jewish grandchildren?' – could be reworded to 'Will we have Catholic or Muslim grandchildren?' and presented by bishops and imams alike.[3] Few religions in Britain can be secure enough to predict the future when so many of their current members are marrying out of the faith.

Alongside the changes in both society and the religious communities, there are important dynamics within the family which can account for mixed-faith marriages. This applies to children who feel that they are so boxed in by the pressures of their family that they cannot define themselves as they wish. The problem may arise because they are an only child – or an eldest child – and they are subject to an enormous amount of expectations that they either cannot live up to or do not wish to live up to. They may find it impossible to negotiate a reasonable compromise or to assert their own identity within the family structure. In the absence of a low-key solution, a dramatic one becomes the only option. The escape route is for them to shatter the framework completely and marry out of the faith – and, in their mind, leap out of the emotional clutches they resent so much. It may not be that it is a deliberate strategy, coldly calculated in advance, but if the circumstances arise then a mixed-faith marriage can seem to be a way of establishing their individuality and allowing them to forge an identity of their own. Mark, now 52, has taken almost twenty years to work out why he was always such an obedient child, teenager and young adult and then suddenly shocked both himself and his family by daring to go out with a non-Baptist and then pressing ahead with their marriage despite the furore it caused: 'It was the first time I really did something for myself. It felt wonderful to be me at last, and I was determined not to let it go.'

Another family pressure can be the role of a child in sustaining the marriage of his/her parents. When all eyes and all conversation revolve on the child and when all communication goes through him – because the marital relationship is defective – the responsibility can be overwhelming. There are numerous ways in which children cope or reject such stresses, but one of them can be to seek to remove themselves as much as possible from them by not only marrying and leaving the home, but by marrying someone who will act as a barrier between them and their parents. Patricia was one such person:

◆ To me, one of the best compliments my mother ever gave Sam when I started bringing him home was 'I don't understand him; we don't seem to speak the same language.' She didn't mean it literally – Sam is a British-born Muslim who speaks impeccable English – but more a matter of not being able to relate to him … which for her meant not being able to dominate him in the way she did me. It was so great to meet someone who wasn't under her spell and couldn't be controlled by her. I felt he was not just my lover, but my protector too.

The fact that a partner has different religious traditions, festivals, foods, home life and family roles can make them especially attractive for those wishing to create an effective buffer zone to ward off their parents. Whether their marriage is successful depends on the strength of the other factors that draw them together.[4]

Within Jewish families, the joke of the Jewish mother-figure can prove much less funny when you have one who is not just overly protective but almost consumes you with care. Rabbi Dow Marmur describes her with precision:

◆ That she wants only the best for her children is beyond question, but it is also self-evident that the outcome for them is too often much less than the best. Too many Jewish women marry their husbands only to fall in love with their sons. The result is that the son has to find the most effective way of getting out of the incestuous (albeit non-sexual) relationship. Frequently, too, he cannot model himself on his father who appears submerged, dominated by his wife. 'Marrying out' is a way of escape and a road to manhood.[5]

In all these instances, mixed-faith relationships can develop not because of cultural integration or religious decline, but as a result of family dynamics which place individuals in a position that they find untenable. In this respect, all faiths are at risk because the root cause lies not in traits unique to any one of them – there are Christian equivalents of the Jewish mother – but in human relationships that get into difficulties.

A different and somewhat paradoxical aspect of family processes is when some individuals marry out of the faith in order to preserve its traditions, according to their view at least. Some Jewish males, for instance, might feel that Jewish women no longer conform to the 'stay at home and look after the children and see to the husband' type, like their mothers did; instead, they are out of the house and busy carving out their own careers. For such males, the choice of a less emancipated Hindu wife who is more likely to take on a submissive and domesticated role has many attractions. Ashley acknowledges that marrying a Hindu means that his children will not have Jewish status, but sees other advantages:

◆ Yes, I know some of my friends think I'm crazy, but in fact I have a much more Jewish-style setup at home than they do. They see their wives by appointment and their children spend more time with the nanny than with their mother. In my house, my wife is always there – for me, for my children, for members of the family who pop by during the day. It's a real home. Obviously it's up to me to provide the Jewish input that she can't, but she creates an environment which matches all the Jewish family values I think used to be so important and which others are missing out on. I know some people think I must be very radical marrying a Hindu, but it's actually because I'm traditional.

Of course, domestic arrangements are often due more to cultural norms than religious beliefs – many Christian wives might have provided Ashley with the *Kinder, Kirche, Küche* lifestyle he prefers – but with members of different religious groups at different stages of cultural patterns, marriage across the religious divide can appear to some as the best way of safeguarding their core values. Sometimes there may also be certain assumptions about other groups that make them appear more attractive than one's own, even though the reality may be different. An example is the reason Millie gave for marrying a Jew rather than a fellow-Catholic: 'Jewish men make better husbands and fathers because they don't beat their wife or children' – a comment whose implications are unfair to many Catholics and unduly complimentary to some Jews, but one that is oft-quoted.

The fourth category of reasons for mixed-faith marriages is the most private: personal factors. These may be affected by external events or other people and may relate to family dynamics, but are specifically personal responses. One is the sense of confused identity that can arise from officially being part of a minority faith-community but not feeling at home in it. If one married a partner of that same faith, the inner conflict would continue. If one married into the Christian majority, one would feel a sense of betrayal – having 'sold out' to the dominant culture – yet not necessarily feel part of that either.

By marrying someone from another minority faith, one is freed from having to fit into the indigenous faith or the surrounding faith. Instead, one is occupying in a religious no-man's-land where one is without pressures or expectations. Aisha, a Muslim, feels that she and her Sikh husband have brought many joys to each other, including a sense of liberation:

◆ Marrying another Muslim would have kept me not knowing who I was, and marrying a Christian was not really on somehow. My husband was in a similar situation. We feel we are able to be ourselves, depart from our respective traditions when we wish, return to them when we wish, and create an atmosphere at home that lets us breathe. Mixing with family can be difficult sometimes, but then it was before we met, which is why I felt the way I did. Am I making myself clear? It's hard to explain sometimes … It's about me being me and being able to sort out what that meant.

Those who are on a journey – be it a search for God or a search for self – will often find that they develop a deep bond with those who are on a similar path. The fact that they come from different religious backgrounds pales into insignificance compared to the common pursuit; it may even be seen as an advantage by those who are concerned with their journey *away* from a tradition as much as that *to* which they are journeying. Those whose use mixed-faith marriage purely as an attempted solution to their identity crisis are in potentially dangerous territory and can find that they have just exchanged one set of problems for another. If, however, there are additional and more positive reasons for their match, then they have every chance of being as successful as any other marriage.

There are also those who consider that the problem with same-faith marriage is not they themselves, but members of the opposite sex within their community. One example is the oft-heard cry of young Jewish men that all eligible Jewish women are demanding, domineering and materialistic. Such women are commonly known as 'Jewish princesses' – on the grounds that their parents treat them like royalty and make it impossible for anything less to satisfy them. The numerous jokes about them portray them as lousy partners, as in 'What does a Jewish princess say when her husband is making love to her? "Darling, the ceiling needs a new coat of paint".' It should be pointed out that this ogre is not nearly as omnipresent as Jewish males complain, and there are many ordinary, unspoilt and caring young Jewish women – but enough of the former exist to tarnish the latter and the myth persists. Frank was very vocal about his experiences:

◆ She was one of those typical Jewish princesses who are only interested in what car you have and what's in your bank account. Dinner together was more like third-degree interrogation. In fact, she was more interested in what my father did than who I was. After two or three dates like that, I thought, 'Right, that's it. I'll be much better off with someone non-Jewish. Somehow non-Jewish girls have a completely different attitude. My mum's furious and Dad wasn't pleased either – though I think he understood.'

No doubt there are situations where this is a fair criticism of the pool of available marriage partners. But sometimes it is very misguided, not only because it lumps all Jewish women in one category, but also because it is more a reflection of that person's own sense of inadequacy. Because they feel unable to achieve certain standards to which they themselves aspire, they blame others for making excessive demands. This might be on a material level, as with Hanif who found that the Sikh women with whom he mixed wanted to marry a businessman or professional, not a carpenter like him, whereas Christian girls seemed to have lower expectations and so he married one. Alternatively, the pressure could operate on a social level, such as being able to repartee with 'loud, vivacious Jewish girls who make me feel I'm chatting up a bulldozer'. This was according to Raymond, who is Jewish, extremely likeable once you get to know him, and very shy. He dutifully tried the Jewish social scene, but felt he was getting nowhere. When he met Susan, a vicar's niece, he was bowled over by her unassuming manner: 'With Susan, I don't feel I have to prove myself. She accepts me for who I am. I can't tell you what a relief that is.'

Raymond has not chosen a mixed-faith partner to deliberately displease his parents, but there are some for whom that is a strong motive. That was the case for Fazal, now known as Frederick: 'I hated Islam being rammed down my throat as a child, and I hated them [my parents] for doing it. It may sound vindictive, but I was determined to marry someone non-Muslim and show them how little it meant to me.' Nicola felt the same way about her religion:

◆ I suppose my parents didn't really deserve it, but as a teenager I was seething with anger. I didn't want to be Jewish, I wished I hadn't been born that way and I was adamant that I was going to get Moses off my back. Marrying in church was the most public way I could do that, although with hindsight I regret the hurt it caused.

In such instances, marrying out was a form of lashing out and an act of rebellion. The target is not always the parents. For Ram it was Sikh society as a whole and a matter of defying the conventions that surrounded him:

◆ I always felt oppressed going to the gurdwara or being involved in communal social gatherings. No one was unpleasant – it just wasn't for me – you could say that mentally I had left the womb and there was no way I could ever fit back in again, or wanted to. I married Christine because we were both medical students and had a lot in common, but it was also a way of letting everyone back in the community know that I was gone for good ... We had a registry office wedding followed by a church blessing. It was supposed to be private with close friends only. I sent invitations to

about 60 people from my parents' community! Christine was horrified, but I knew that not a single one would attend, and none of
them did. The invites were farewell cards really.

It is likely that the number of mixed-faith marriages motivated
wholly or partially out of the 'rebellion motive' declines the
more integrated is the religious community in wider society.
For those that are fairly insular and cut off from wider currents,
choosing a partner from beyond those frontiers is a potent act
and a good way of sticking two fingers up at those from whom
you wish to dissociate. When the dividing lines are more fluid
and there is greater interchange with society at large, the act of
outmarriage loses its force and the need to take such a startling
course is less necessary; in those circumstances, moreover,
there are many other ways of slipping into mainstream society.
As a generalization, individuals who intermarry as an act of
rebellion are largely found among the first generation of those
who intermarry, while they are less common amongst subsequent generations.

A factor that is much more persistent is the sexual one. The
physical attraction of men and women from different religious
and cultural groups to one's own can be very enticing. 'Hindu
women are so sublime; their bodies so female' said Gary, while
Caroline had fantasies about Muslim males 'whose bodies reek
of manhood unlike all the C. of E. wimps I meet at the office.'
Jewish men and Christian women have long held a special place
in each other's sexual psyches. Some Jewish males lust after
'big blondes' and take it for granted that they are much better
in bed. The assumption is that Jewish women are too nice, and
that good sex involves rough play and dirty doings; Jewish girls
may make great mothers, but '*shikses* are better between the
sheets'. For their part, some Christian women are stimulated
by the image of the Jewish male, whose swarthiness makes him
desirable and whose circumcision is especially tantalizing. The
sexual attraction on both sides is also heightened by the lure of

the exotic and the delight of forbidden fruits. Kate was very candid about her feelings:

◆ As the child of a fairly strict Presbyterian household – almost to the point of being asexual – I was yearning to be sexually emancipated. At college I slept around a bit but never felt anyone was really touching me properly. I began to think maybe sex wasn't that great in the first place and was just all hyped up. Meeting Yaqub was like a bombshell. I virtually had an orgasm just looking at him. We were in bed within five minutes … well, maybe that's an exaggeration, but later that day anyway. I still can't take my hands off him after three years of marriage. Some of my more daring friends say 'Muslims are circumcised aren't they – what's it like?' And I usually reply 'Best of all!'

Logic plays very little part in such attraction of opposites. The Jewish girls whom Jewish males reject can be highly prized by others. As Saul Bitensky writes:

◆ There are non-Jewish men whose dream girl is an exotic princess of otherness from London NW6. They don't look at Jewish girls the way we do. They see a Jewess – a Mediterranean maiden.'[6]

Beauty is in the eye of the beholder and passion is often hidden in mixed-faith loincloths.

A much more altruistic motive that can lead to a mixed-faith marriage is a desire to change the world. It stems from the deeply held conviction that one of the ways that individuals can bring peace to our war-ravaged planet is by breaking down as many social and religious barriers as possible. Governments may control major events on the world-stage, but bit-players have an important role too; ordinary people can slowly eradicate the climate of hate and suspicion upon which conflicts feed. Simon did not consciously seek a non-Catholic bride, but when he met Usha he was delighted:

◆ Obviously I married her because I loved her. But I also think it's enormously important to have marriages like ours – a white Catholic and a brown Hindu – because it says to the rest of the world 'Look, differences are surmountable – in fact, they don't matter at all – it's people that count, not the place in which they were born, or the colour of their skin, or the strangeness of their beliefs'. And I think it will be the best lesson in life that we can give our children – that Mummy and Daddy could have been living in different housing estates that were no-go areas for each other's residents, but instead are cooking dinner together in the same kitchen.

This mixed-faith menu to save the world – religious curry and chips – may indeed help disseminate a more tolerant approach; but if, as can happen, the children have relatively little religious education and the parents are more interested in political activities and social action, then the attempt to produce greater religious understanding and harmony inevitably peters out.

The final aspect in this list of personal factors behind mixed-faith marriages is perhaps the most significant in contributing to the rising numbers – divorce. Research has shown that the previous marital status of a person can affect their likelihood of marrying out of the faith. A study in Indiana in 1963, for instance, revealed that the intermarriage rate for those who had previously been widowed was 20%, while for those never married before it was 33.2%, and for those previously divorced it was 64.9%. There are several reasons why widows and widowers are the most likely to remarry within the faith: because, assuming their first marriage was a successful one, they wish to replicate it as much as possible, which includes a same-faith partner; because they usually maintain their existing social circle, which can often be amongst same-faith individuals or even part of a religious community, and are therefore likely to find a new partner from within that group; because if widowed at a young age with children still at home, they may feel it is particularly important to carry on the religious traditions in which they have been brought up and so will prefer to enter a same-faith marriage; because the majority tend to be widowed at a late age and therefore be more conservative about marriage patterns and consider it either wrong or inappropriate to marry someone of a different faith.

For those who have been divorced, the situation is often entirely the opposite and they are the most likely to marry out of the faith. In their case, there are even more reasons for doing so than those previously single: first the hostility against their former partner may be transferred to anything which symbolized them – be it their family, their friends, their favourite food (even though it could have been enjoyed by both of them) and their religion (even though they both shared the same faith). As Mike put it, 'I know that I am as Jewish as is Carol, my "ex" – so it wasn't "her thing" – but somehow Jewish food and family and festivals is all tied up with her in my mind and I don't want any of it any more.' Second, the break in the marriage is often accompanied by a break with the mutual friends the couple once had. Both seek out new social circles, and the ones where they are less likely to meet each other or bump into old acquaintances will tend to be general leisure groups, evening classes, sports clubs and singles groups in which there is no common religious denomination. Thirdly, the sale of the marital home and the search for cheaper property by one or both partners may lead either of them to move out of the area and to settle in a totally new environment where there may not be many members of their own faith-community. Fourthly, it is much harder establishing a new social life once a person has left the age of youth clubs and college societies, when most of one's friends are single too and are a source of introduction to new faces. Having to look for a partner is difficult enough for any divorcee, even if they are part of the religious and cultural majority. When they are part of a religious minority it restricts the pool of eligible partners considerably; even locating available partners in the first place is a major difficulty, quite apart from whether one finds any of them suitable. By deciding to enter a mixed-faith relationship, one is expanding one's horizon enormously and increasing one's prospects of success. As Ali said succinctly, 'For every Muslim woman I might meet, there are thirty non-Muslims. It would be daft to limit my options so severely.'

A fifth reason is that many divorcees feel that they played by the rules the first time, by marrying within the faith, but it did not work and so they are free to change the rules next time round. Janice spoke for countless others of all faiths when she said: 'I did everything by the book when I was married and it all ended in tears. Being both Jewish didn't stop us tearing each other to bits. So maybe now I'll have better luck with someone out of the faith – it certainly can't be any worse.' Henry – who met his wife in the church bell-ringing group – felt similarly: 'Although I entered my first marriage willingly, I was conscious that it was what everyone else in the family wanted – right sort of girl and all that – and what I had been groomed for. Next time I marry, it'll be purely up to me. It's my turn now.' A sixth cause is that divorcees have been living away from the parental home for several years and used to running their own life. They are therefore older and more independent than those marrying for the first time, who may still be living with their parents or more subject to their influence. The family pressures to marry within the faith are considerably lessened, and even if they still do exist, divorcees feel more able to resist them. Mary relates how her parents put an end to a serious relationship with a non-Catholic before she married her Catholic ex-husband. 'Now I don't think they'd dare say anything, and even if they did they would get short shrift from me.'

A seventh reason lies with the religious communities themselves, who sometimes fail to provide the support that is needed by divorcees and newly created single-parent families. 'It was awful,' said Susie. 'One moment I was really involved in synagogue life, the next I was social outcast number one.'

Matthew had a similar experience with his church:

◆ Suddenly it was as if I didn't exist. The vicar mumbled something about having a chat one day and avoided me thereafter, and everyone else treated me as a leper. Half the men thought I would now be after their wives – a rogue male rampaging around the church – while the women thought it would give their menfolk bad ideas. Honestly, the small-mindedness was incredible. It was not as if I was a stranger they didn't know. And you would have thought that being a religious organization they would have been the ones full of compassion and care. I felt I never wanted to go there again. In fact I don't.

Others may not feel rejected in such a direct way, but will slip out of contact for different reasons. It may be because they have been badly hurt by the divorce and simply want to avoid large social gatherings. Typical comments are 'I couldn't face being with others' or 'I didn't want to have to explain why my husband doesn't come any more over and over again.' Alternatively they may have felt too self-conscious, like Sheila, who reported: 'I made an effort to go along, but I felt I stuck out like a sore thumb. They may not have all been looking at me, but I certainly felt they were.' Many were aware that religious institutions tended to cater for couples and felt that they no longer qualified. As Rosie said:

◆ The norm in our synagogue is the stereotype happy family of husband, wife and two children. For years I was part of that and so it never bothered me. Now that I am by myself, I have suddenly realized how off-putting that is to anyone not in that category. And although the rabbi is very nice and says I am just as welcome as before, I feel that I'm intruding. Maybe it's all in my own head, but it's as if I'm the spectre at the feast and a ghastly reminder of what can go wrong in life.

Others were taken aback by the lack of pastoral care. Karen had been a weekly churchgoer for years, but had stopped for a few weeks once the divorce became public. She was about to return to church when 'it hit me – no one had taken the trouble to ring or see how I was; if I meant that little to them, then what was the point? I never did go back.'

An additional problem is faced by Catholics, the teachings of whose faith are steadfastly opposed to divorce. When they feel that the condition of the marriage leaves them with no option but to get divorced – or if they are presented with divorce by their spouse against their will – the religious implications can have a traumatic effect. However much the divorce is necessary, or beyond their control, they may still feel in a state of sin vis-à-vis the Church and feel obliged not to participate in communal affairs. As Helen explained:

◆ I was a stalwart of the community, not just going to Mass regularly, but taking part in everything from the flower arrangements to the annual fair. When I got divorced I felt awful. I know how much the Church frowns on it and there I was, flouting its teachings. The priest was very kind but I knew it put him in an impossible position, and I thought the best thing was for me to opt out.

The Church of England is less hostile towards divorce, but will not usually marry a divorcee in church if their former spouse is still living. This, too, can cause embarrassment, or resentment, to those recently divorced who feel that they live under a cloud of disapproval and have a second-class status. Barry was both cross and hurt:

◆ I was in church on an ordinary Sunday morning when I realized that of all the other single people there, I was the only one who the vicar would not marry. That really upset me. I also felt angry that if I ever did want to remarry, then at the time when I needed the Church most, it would turn its back on me. That's not very Christian is it?

In all these different cases, there is a direct relationship between those who divorce and those who marry out of the faith. The teachings of the religion and the response of community members (or their lack of response) mean that divorcees who were previously involved in communal life feel disinclined to continue. Whether they were pushed away or just crept away unnoticed, the net result was that they left the same-faith circles in which they had mixed and were much more likely to develop new contacts outside of the faith. In some instances, it was even an advantage to marry out of the faith and not face the problem of having to approach their minister again. With the divorce rate in Britain already high and continuing to increase, that in itself is one reason to expect the intermarriage rate to grow too.

Four overall categories have been identified so far, relating to wider society, the religious communities, family dynamics, and personal factors. There is also a fifth aspect that is not so easy to analyse but must be mentioned – chance. There are many individuals who did not enter a mixed-faith marriage for any of the numerous reasons listed above, but simply because 'it just happened that way.' Many of the relationships resulted from chance meetings when they were not looking for romance – waiting at a taxi rank or after asking someone for directions. Moreover, it could be at a time when normally they were not exposed to mixed-faith social circles or when they were already going out with someone of their own faith. 'It was a matter of sheer luck that we even spoke to each other,' said Kitty. 'It was only because I missed a train and then happened to stand next to Bill at the information desk. Otherwise our worlds would never have met.' The chance factor is seen in families of all faiths in which siblings have had the same religious upbringing, cultural condition and parental influence, yet have followed radically different marriage patterns. Howard and Jeff are brothers, just over two years apart in age and come from a close and warm Jewish family. Howard surprised no one by marrying a Jewish girl, but Jeff shocked everyone when he married out of the faith. There was no particular reason for such a different result: 'I had gone out mainly with Jewish girls before I met my wife. We just met at a business conference and to my amazement things took off from there.'

Jeff's case also highlights another common feature – that mixed-faith marriages can not only amaze the family, but can take the person involved by surprise too. 'I knew it would be difficult telling my parents,' said Tracy, 'but the hardest part was telling myself. I kept on thinking – this isn't happening to me – not me.' For many in this position, marrying out of the faith was not just unintentional, but it also went against their own principles. 'Whenever discussions came up about inter-marriage, it was always me who said how wrong it was', recalls Tracy. Her attitude was echoed by many others, including Rosalind who said:

◆ This may sound daft, but even though I am in a mixed-faith marriage, and a very happy one at that, I still feel it's better not to have them. Okay, our marriage works marvellously, and I hope it will continue this way for the rest of my life, but I think the potential problems are enormous. So I would still counsel people against it in principle.

This disapproval of the very course that they themselves had taken was evident also in their hopes for their children. Stuart's comments typified those of many: 'I may have married out of the faith, but however hypocritical this may seem, I still want my children to marry within the faith. I just think it's better that way for all the usual reasons.' There may be a certain amount of guilt in statements like this, trying to ensure that the continuity of faith that they have put at risk is guaranteed by the children marrying back into the fold. This would exonerate them from criticism over undermining the faith and relieve them of all the 'I told you so' comments from relatives. But whatever their motives, they cannot really be accused of hypocrisy – for that would imply pretending to take a view to which they did not actually subscribe. Jeff, Rosalind, Stuart and many others were genuinely against the idea of mixed-faith marriage – but life turned out different.

Notes

1 Daiches, David, *Two Worlds*, New York, Harcourt Brace & Co, 1954, p. 183

2 Barbara, Augustin, *Mixed Marriages (Some Key Questions)*, Paper delivered to the Conference of the International Union of Family Organizations on 'Marriage across Frontiers' at Newcastle, Northern Ireland, 18–21 May 1992, p. 13; Brandeis Research Project on Intermarriage, quoted in *The American Jewish Yearbook*, New York, 1992; Stringer, Peter, 'Cross-community marriage in Northern Ireland: social support and social constraints', *Sexual and Marital Therapy*, vol. 9, No. 1, 1994, pp. 74, 82

3 Sacks, Jonathan, *Will We Have Jewish Grandchildren?*, London, Vallentine Mitchell & Co, 1994

4 For a further examination of these aspects, see Friedman, E.H., 'The Myth of the Shiksa' in McGoldrick, M., Pearce, J.K. and Giordiano J. (eds), *Ethnicity and Family Therapy*, New York, The Guildford Press, 1982

5 Marmur, Dow, 'Intermarriage', London, Reform Synagogues of Great Britain, 1973, p. 6

6 *New Moon*, London, December 1994, p. 23

Chapter Four

Avoiding a divorce before the wedding

What happens during the courtship,
and when the engagement is announced,
and on the wedding day

'Of all the disasters that could befall us in future years, the one thing that never worries me is getting divorced – if we managed to survive the courtship, everything after that will be a piece of cake.' It is not just what Neil says that is so striking but the forcefulness with which he says it, spitting out the words as if he was trying to physically blot out all memory of those times. 'It was horrendous,' agrees his wife. 'There was so much criticism from his parents. What should have been a really romantic time was like being in a boxing ring dodging all the blows that came our way.' Their experience is not true of all mixed-faith relationships; some couples do not face problems at all, with their parents either delighted with the match or less sure, but feeling that they must let the couple sort out their own destiny and not interfere. Other couples report that the only comment is when the engagement is announced, where-upon one parent briefly mutters 'You sure you think it's all right, being different religions and all that?' and, once reassured, the champagne bottles are uncorked. This chapter, though, will concentrate on the difficulties, because for those families who do encounter them, they can cause much heartache and soul-searching.

Neil's story is representative of those where one set of parents objected and the other did not. Being Jewish, his family expected him to go out only with Jewish girls. Charlotte was from a lapsed Church of England family. To his parents, though, it was no different from her being a bishop's daughter – she was not Jewish and that was that. When Neil first told his parents about her he was met with stony silence, although that was quickly followed by a series of accusations: 'How can you do this to us? Doesn't your heritage mean anything to you? Do you know it will break your grandmother's heart?' Over the next few weeks he was constantly asked: 'When are you going to bring home a nice Jewish girl?' On one occasion Neil replied in exasperation, 'I don't know any nice Jewish girls', only to be told, 'Then bring home a horrible Jewish girl.' They were not joking. As the relationship progressed and was clearly becoming serious, the comments became more barbed about the long-term success: 'Do you really think it will work? You can't marry chalk and cheese. It's got no future' followed up by the classic threat: 'You wait till your first argument and she turns round and says "You bloody Jew!" – then how will you feel?' In Daniel's case it was his two brothers who objected the most when he, from a closely-knit Catholic family, started dating Nancy, a Protestant girl. After rows in the home failed to persuade Daniel to break off the relationship, a group of his brother's friends took to trailing him in the High Street with jeers and catcalls. Nancy was followed too and on three occasions jostled and physically intimidated. Aziz also faced regular physical threats from a zealous member of the local mosque when he was seen with a Christian girl. The harassment reached such an extent that he eventually obtained a restraining order from the courts ordering that person not to come near the two of them again.

Minesh did not even have the luxury of walking in the street with his non-Hindu girlfriend. He was well aware of how much his parents would disapprove and felt it necessary to hide the relationship from them. When four years later he announced they were to marry, 'it was like World War Two – we rowed for hours and they were so furious that I had to leave the house that night. After that I left home as soon as I could and rented a room till we could both get a place together. It was awful and I prefer not to think about those days too much.' Surinda also did not tell his parents about his non-Sikh girlfriend. In his case, however, they found out about the relationship after a few months:

◆ They gave me hell. So I pretended to split up, but in fact we carried on together. It was very difficult – both deceiving my parents and not being able to do normal things with my girlfriend openly together. After two years I felt I couldn't go on this way – and it wasn't much fun for her either – we had to go public. Of course, there was a bit of an explosion to put it mildly, but at least it was out in the open and we weren't keeping secrets any more. They still didn't come to the wedding – but at least I could tell them about plans and let them know what was going on.

Jira faced a double problem. She was in love with a Christian boyfriend, a relationship which her Muslim parents refused to countenance. In any case, they had decided upon an arranged marriage with someone from Pakistan whom she had not met. She was distraught at the prospect and ran away with her boyfriend, whom she married shortly afterwards without their knowledge. She has not seen her parents in the three years since then, and communicates only through occasional letters. She would like to meet them and introduce her husband, but is not hopeful about the prospects.

Some couples find that they are fighting on all fronts, with both sets of parents voicing objections. Roy was Jewish and Tina was Catholic, and both lived in Liverpool. When they went out together, there were a few murmurings from both sides, but when they said they intended getting engaged, the four parents got together and agreed that it must not proceed. They were very united in their opposition! Thus far the story is typical of many mixed-faith relationships that were halted before any rings were bought and never went any further. The result sometimes is that the respective partners do go on to each find suitable partners within their own faith. In other cases, one or both of the former partners meet up with yet another person from outside their faith, decide that they are not giving up love for duty a second time, and proceed with the relationship irrespective of parental finger-wagging. The particular story of Roy and Tina is worth pursuing because of what happened later. Despite being very much in love, the couple reluctantly agreed to separate and shortly afterwards Roy moved down to London. There he met a Jewish girl, married her and they had two children. After a while the marriage became very rocky and eventually resulted in divorce. Some time later Roy had to go to Liverpool on business. His trip took him past the house where Tina had lived and, for nostalgia's sake, he stopped and knocked on the door to see what had happened to the family. To his surprise Tina opened the door. She was still single. They quickly struck up their relationship again and this time decided not to let external factors impede their togetherness. They are now married, are very happy, and their only regret is the eleven years that they spent needlessly apart.

Whilst every mixed-faith couple has to cope with a slightly different set of circumstances, a trait common to many is that they date each other for much longer than do those not facing such problems. Several tell of relationships lasting seven to ten years before they announced their engagement, largely because it took that long to gain the family's approval, or at least to mitigate their outright opposition. Maneh went out with his non-Hindu girlfriend for nine years before he felt his parents had accepted her sufficiently for him to plan a wedding. Darren's parents let their feelings be known in no uncertain terms when he told them he was going out with Susan, who was non-Jewish. Nevertheless he continued with her and they eventually started living together. He still went home to his parents every Friday night for the traditional Sabbath eve meal, but they never invited Susan and he felt unable to bring her. For ten years he left her alone every Friday night until one day he decided:

◆ It was crunch time. I had to confront them and say: 'Look, Susan and I are together and you either have to accept us both or do without me.' There was a deathly hush and then my mother said: 'Why don't you bring Susan with you next Friday?' Part of me was very relieved, because it could have gone the other way and ended in me storming out; but I was also angry too. Here I was, always a very good and caring son, and it had taken them ten years to accept the person I was in love with. If things had been different we would have been married years ago. We could have had three children by now, instead we were just getting round to talking about the wedding reception.

The transition from going out together and being engaged can be surprisingly traumatic. Zoe was staggered by her parents 'who knew we'd been together for three years and never said a word, but went berserk when I said we were getting engaged'. The best explanation is that parents who either turn a blind eye to mixed-faith dating, or who hope that it will end in tears of its own accord, are suddenly confronted by the hard reality of the relationship turning into a permanent fixture, and they then voice the hostility that they had previously muffled. Philip's father had always welcomed his girlfriend into the house and been friendly to her, but the moment they announced plans to marry he banned her from the house. Doris' mother made their opposition clear in a different way: 'I just stood there and

wept when my mother refused to look at my engagement ring.'
Many other young couples were caught by surprise similarly,
expecting beaming congratulations but receiving stony looks
instead. Twenty-eight years afterwards, Barbara can 'still feel
the hurt when I announced my engagement and my father said
it was the worst day of his life.' Some parents not only rejected
their offspring's prospective partner, but also their offspring.
Whatever faith they may be, some parents feel torn but ultimately without any choice, like Tevye, the traditional Jew grap-
pling with a changing world in the musical *Fiddler on the Roof*:

On the one hand, can I deny everything I believe in?
On the other hand, can I deny my daughter?
On the one hand, can I turn my back on my faith?
On the other hand … there is no other hand!

As a result of this self-dialogue he pushes his daughter away
and refuses to acknowledge her existence any more. It was an
accurate portrayal of ghetto life 100 years ago, but some real-
life parents still do the same. A well-known public example is
the father of Edwina Currie M.P. who never spoke to her after
she became engaged to a non-Jew, and died four years after
their wedding without ever having met his first grandchild. A
similar response from a different tradition led a Sikh father to
tear up all photographs of his daughter when she married out
of the religion and ban her from ever entering the house again.
In some cases, there is the additional motive of trying to
prevent younger offspring from following the example of the
sibling who is marrying out; they are shown in the most drastic
way possible the censure that would befall them should they
cross the religious frontier in the same way.

Whatever the religion to which the parents belong, those
adamantly opposed to intermarriage often seem to adopt a
similar strategy in trying to separate the newly engaged
couples. Among them are:

1 Prevent them meeting again, whether by forbidding them verbally or by sending them abroad (such as to visit relatives in India, or to work on kibbutz in Israel).

2 Create obstacles ('you won't marry till you buy a house' – hoping that by the time they can afford one the relationship will have cooled; or 'you must bring her to synagogue/ the gurdwara – hoping the experience will deter the other partner).

3 Criticize the other person's suitability (can equally be 'he's not good enough for you' or 'he's too good for you').

4 Instil a sense of guilt ('it will kill your grandfather if we tell him'; 'all our sacrifices for you seem in vain'; '2000 years of tradition will cease because of you').

5 Give direct threats ('she will never step inside this house'; 'you'll be cut out of the will'; 'we won't come to the wedding').

6 Predict a terrible future ('it can't possibly work'; 'he won't treat you the way you expect'; 'her family will take over and dominate your home').

7 Enlist others to dissuade the person (usually relatives or the minister, although sometimes trying to get friends 'to make him see sense' and sometimes contacting the other parents to see if they are potential allies).

It is noticeable that these and many other strategies are employed as much by parents who have little religious involvement as by those who are staunchly traditional. Many of their objections are triggered by an emotional reaction rather than a concern for theology. One is a sense of rejection: that by marrying 'somebody different from us' their child is turning his/her back on them and it is perceived as a slap in the face. Another is worry that the new partner will cause their son or daughter to become alienated from them. As Annie said: 'I'm sure my daughter-in-law will drag my son away from us. I can feel it in my bones.' There is also a guilt at 'where did we go wrong?' and a deep sense of failure that all the time and effort they put in their child's upbringing has been wasted. For some parents there is anger that they are being shamed. 'How can my son do this to me when he knows I'll never be able to show my face in church again?' said one distraught mother. It begs the question of whether she really is responsible for her son's choice of marriage partner, and whether it is right that fellow congregants should spurn her rather than support her. Other parents are more bothered by the thought of having grandchildren of a different faith to them. This can either be because they fear a lack of relationship – 'they'll think of us as strangers' – or because they feel that their family line will now come to an end and that they will lose their stake in the future.

In some cases, those fears may be justified. It is certainly true that for those who wish to hurt their parents, the best way is to reject their God and their belief-system. However, in the vast majority of cases, those worries are misplaced. The offspring see no contradiction between loving their parents and loving their different-faith partner, and are hurt by the suggestion that there is a clash or that they have to choose between the two of them. Conversely, the partners are usually very keen to get to know the family of the person they love and to be welcomed by them. Moreover, if the channels of communication are good, the parents can have a very positive input into the new couple's home and play a helpful role in passing on their traditions to any grandchildren. It is ironic that some parents cause their worst fears to come true by pushing away their child and/or partner to such an extent that they ensure the new couple become ostracized from them. Another source of friction can be when there is disagreement between the parents themselves. In the not uncommon case of Millie and Bertram, he was adamant that their non-Jewish daughter-in-law should not step inside the house, while she was equally disappointed at the match but felt that an open-door policy was best. Their hurt at the mixed-faith marriage was compounded by the strife that it sparked between the two of them.

In cases where one partner is Jewish there are often two additional factors at work. One is that the Jewish parents feel guilty that they who survived the Holocaust are now witnessing another 'final solution' to the continuity of the Jewish people that is less evil but perhaps more effective. Whether they themselves lost relatives or not, they sense the burden of history and feel that they are betraying the memory of the six million Jews who were murdered by letting their son/daughter marry out of the faith. Conversely, some non-Jewish parents can oppose the match because of anti-Semitism. This may be because they themselves are anti-Semitic – whether 'in a mild sort of way' or virulently prejudiced – and are horrified at the thought of a Jew becoming part of their family. Alternatively, they may have no qualms of their own accord, but are afraid of other people's anti-Semitism and how that may affect their child and future grandchildren. Max had no objections to his Jewish son-in-law and welcomed him wholeheartedly, but he was afraid that 'marrying him puts my daughter in the front line', while he was also concerned because 'I know the sorts of names that can be used in school playgrounds about Jews and it worries me that any children they have will be exposed to that sort of thing'.

Similar fears and prejudices can operate when a mixed-faith marriage is also a mixed-colour one. When Clare, a white Church of England girl, brought home her black Muslim boyfriend, it was skin-pigmentation rather than religious differences that most alarmed her parents:

◆ It was body language at its best. When I told them in advance he wasn't Christian, they raised their eyebrows, but when he came through the door their mouths dropped open. Looking back, it was quite amusing but at the time I was too nervous to appreciate that … After he had gone my dad turned round to me and said,

'You can't be serious.' When I accused him of being prejudiced, he said it wasn't a matter of prejudice, but of like marrying like. Of course, religion didn't come up once in the conversation they had with him. Even if he'd been a black Christian they'd still have taken the same attitude.

Her experience was not an isolated one. Several white families who referred to 'cultural problems' with their child's partner really meant 'colour problems'. They were either too embarrassed to say so outright, or had not even acknowledged to themselves the latent racism that lay behind their objections. But prejudice is not the monopoly of majority cultures; minorities can be equally insular. Martin did not expect his Jewish parents to be pleased about his girlfriend, who was not only from a Sikh family but very dark-skinned, but he was unprepared for the extent of their reaction:

◆ They went ballistic. It was incredible. It was as if I was marrying Hitler's daughter. But it was all to do with her colour. When I said that Jews should be the last people to be racist after all we'd suffered from others, they just said that if it was racist not to want coffee-coloured grandchildren, then they were racist. To give them credit, when they calmed down they admitted it was unfair to react that way, but said that was the way they felt and they couldn't be reasonable about emotions.

In some instances, the parental horror can be reciprocated, with coloured Muslim or Hindu families being as much bothered by the white skin of their in-laws as by their different faith. Marvin and Jean are committed members of a black evangelical church and they were appalled when their daughter became seriously involved with a Catholic who was white. They, too, were influenced by colour rather than theology, and lectured their daughter not about the brotherhood of Christ but how white men rape black women. It should be pointed out that not everyone is racist and there are mixed-faith and mixed-colour marriages that receive the support of both families. Yet even they would admit that it can be a double handicap in certain situations. Britain may be a multi-religious and multi-racial society, but it is not yet an unprejudiced society, and such couples can be exposed to discrimination from all quarters, expected and unexpected.

Anguish and arguments may well precede many marriages, but ultimately an increasing number of today's parents find they not only have little control over their children's paths, but are not prepared to cut off all contact in the name of tradition. This is true not only of religiously lapsed parents, but also of those who are still committed. It reflects two social factors: first, that the tendency to have smaller families than in previous generations means that casting out a child is a much harder step. Losing one child out of eight is sad, but losing one out of two is unbearable. Secondly, the fact that children marry at an older age and have often left home before marrying gives them an independence that lessens the impact of parental threats of dissociation. Love-struck seventeen-year-olds can have their pocket money stopped and sent to their room; twenty-seven-year-olds living in a semi-detached twenty miles away, who are used to making decisions in every other aspect of their life, will do so in the question of marriage too. Once all parental attempts to postpone the relationship have failed (or have not even been implemented for fear of being counterproductive), reluctant acceptance is the general reaction. In this respect, parents are the mirror image of their children, who in choosing their partner also put feelings before faith.

Time can prove a healer, and whilst some parents disapprove of the new member of the family in principle because of his/her faith, as they come to know them they grow to like them as an individual. The oft-heard comment 'I couldn't wish for a better daughter-in-law, if only she were Jewish, she'd be perfect' is said more as a compliment than a complaint.

Sometimes the path to reconciliation can take many years. John, a committed Baptist, was deeply disturbed by his daughter's marriage to a Hindu and made his views known to them. It took five years before he saw them regularly, but now he admits that he has grown to love and respect his Hindu son-in-law: 'Gradually I came to realize that the problem was me, not them.' For other parents there is always a tinge of regret. In the words of Zaki, a Muslim whose son has married a Sikh: 'I have accepted it, but deep down I have not accepted it.' The difference between approval and acceptance is a painful lesson that many a parent has had to master. The age of the 'child' can also be a factor in the parents' change of heart. Most parents wish to see their offspring married. If their son or daughter is of an age at which they begin to worry that he/she will never find a partner and settle down, the fact that the spouse turns out to be of a different faith becomes less unacceptable. Charlie spoke for many parents when he said, 'At the end of the day, I'm not going to be around for ever and I want my daughter to be with someone she can trust and who will take good care of her. That's got to be the priority hasn't it?'

A minority of parents who are strongly opposed to the union neither accept it nor break off contact but continue the religious war through constant criticism or seeking to magnify problems. As with any marital issue in which there is hostile parental interference, the result is often very distressing. Bakhshish's parents could not come to terms with his non-Sikh bride and regularly harangued him over the matter:

◆ I dreaded the phone ringing and hated visits home. It was just awful. Nothing positive and everything thrown at us. I told them time and again I had made my decision and nothing would alter it, but they took no notice. After a few months I told my wife she shouldn't come with me on the visits any more, because I didn't want her to be in the firing line. I kept going out of loyalty, but in the end it became too much. I told my parents to either stop or be prepared to say goodbye to me. It worked for a week and then started up all over again. I haven't spoken to them for two years now, though I do keep in touch with my three brothers and one sister.

There is no doubt that parents should feel free to express their opinions. Parents have rights too, including the right to urge what they see as their child's best interests, whatever the issue and however old is the 'child'. Moreover, they may be able to point out aspects of the relationship that the couple had not considered. The wisest course for parents is to observe three guidelines. First, that when they raise reservations they do so constructively and in a way that does not involve abusive language. In this way, not only is their advice more likely to be heard, but it will not jeopardize relations with the couple if the marriage proceeds. As Hannah knows only too well, 'Even though my parents eventually accepted our marriage, so many nasty things had been said beforehand that it soured everything and we have never been as close as we could have been.' Second, that there is a dividing line, perhaps at the point of marriage itself: beforehand it is legitimate to voice anxieties and raise question marks, and thereby influence what takes place; after that moment it is time to come to terms with reality, however much it is disliked, and learn to live with a *fait accompli*. The third rule is to keep the channels of communication open, so that even if differences cannot be resolved and certain conversation points have to be avoided, both sides stay in touch and the parents gradually build up a relationship with the son/daughter-in-law they did not want but have to accept.

When it is just one set of parents who object to the relationship, it can not only be very hurtful to the couple but also to the other set of parents. Harry and Kit were staggered by what happened when their daughter became engaged:

◆ We were delighted. We'd always liked Adrian and always made him feel welcome. But his parents – goodness gracious – they were not at all pleased and raised all sorts of objections. At the bottom of it all was that our daughter was not Jewish. Well, I have to tell you that, Jewish or not, she is universally liked and you couldn't want a kinder and more warm-hearted girl. But that obviously wasn't good enough for them. After the initial shock, we got very angry: what right had they to say she was not good enough and unsuitable? It was untrue and it was insulting. And what did it say about us and the way we had brought her up?

Rita and Bernard – nominal Catholics – were equally miffed by the hostile reaction their son received from his prospective Muslim in-laws: 'I suppose it was a double hurt – being told that our son was undesirable when we know he is a super chap, and knowing that when the marriage did go ahead, we were not going to have any relationship with our in-laws. It's desperately sad.' In cases such as these, it was generally the parents of the partner who came from the more minority religion that had the most reservations. Whilst this is almost inevitable – those being the parents who generally had the greater religious attachment and who were most afraid of children losing their identity – it often led to charges of inverted prejudice. Among Rita's comments were 'If we said half the things about them that they said about us, we'd be accused of racism!' Harry made a similar point about his daughter's in-laws when he stated, 'If I rejected their son on grounds of being the wrong religion, it would be counted as anti-Semitic. So how come it's okay for them to reject my daughter?'

Parents are not the only source of contention. Grandparents often have stronger religious views than the parents of the couple – particularly among the minority faiths, as they are less assimilated in wider society. In certain families, it is their opinion that carries greater weight. In many instances they can take a divergent view from the parents – objecting when the latter are accepting, or vice versa. Jane's parents did not mind too much when she married a non-Catholic, but her grandmother was desperately upset, refused to attend the wedding and had not yet seen her two-year-old grandson. Ross was very taken aback that his grandparents criticized him over his non-Jewish fiancée: 'I was used to arguing with my parents – that was normal – but I was always very close to my grandad and ma. When they turned on me, that really hurt.' At other times, it is the grandparents who can have a healing role, 'knocking sense' into parents and children, helping both sides to keep everything in perspective and not forget the bonds of affection that unite them. This is also true of siblings. Being of the same generation as the person marrying out of the faith, they are well aware of the social currents that have led to the relationship, yet also appreciate the upset that the parents feel. Often they occupy the role of middlemen, urging each party to understand the position of the other, or even act as go-betweens, negotiating terms by which 'Mum and Dad will invite Mike's fiancée round and he will talk to her about having the wedding in a registry office rather than in church'. In some cases, though, brothers and sisters can be equally disapproving, whether it is because they object to mixed-faith marriages in principle or because they are aware of the distress caused to their parents by it. As was seen above, when Bakhshish broke off relations with his parents, he kept contact with his siblings. Abdul, however, lost his whole family. His brother and sister were still living at home when he married a non-Muslim whereupon his parents declared him *persona non grata* and forbade them to have any further contact with him.

The role of friends can vary too. Normally they are supportive, precisely because they are friends and share the same perspective. Many couples can attest to how good it was to have friends with whom to mull over problems when relations with their family were going through a difficult stage.

However, there are also those who have been surprised by the reaction of friends, as in the case of Juliette:

◆ My two best friends were Jewish like me and we'd stuck together through all the different boyfriends we'd had. We'd cried together and laughed together over them, and it was great. But that changed when I started dating Bill, who was not Jewish. They were really disapproving. I couldn't believe it. And when I introduced them to him and asked them about him afterwards, there was this stony silence as if to say 'you've broken the rules'. The more serious Bill and I got, the more the gulf grew. By the time we were engaged I hardly saw them. There was no point inviting them to the wedding – they wouldn't have come. I suppose it was good preparation for some of the problems we faced, but I'm still amazed and I feel they let me down very badly.

The other main players in the life-drama of mixed-faith couples, especially when planning the wedding, are the clergy. They more than anyone else can produce diverse reactions, ranging from fear to hero worship to contempt to despair. The fact that three out of four of these feelings are negative is a reflection of the general pattern, with ministers of all faiths being largely opposed to such marriages. Some are so forthright in their condemnation that the couple do not even bother to approach them – or dare to. As Hayley put it: 'I would rather walk down Oxford Street during the rush hour completely naked than tell my priest that I'm engaged to a non-Catholic.' Leslie was a little braver and telephoned his rabbi to see what he had to say – but the rabbi put the phone down on him the moment he heard it was a mixed marriage. The majority of ministers will at least meet with the couple, either to tell them why they should separate or to point out the many pitfalls ahead. As was seen earlier, mixed-faith marriages cannot take place in synagogue for legal reasons. The Buddhist, Hindu, Muslim, and Sikh communities in Britain do not have the right to conduct wedding ceremonies that have legal status, and so may only hold services after a civil marriage has taken place. If a Muslim minister feels that the other partner will join, or at least support, the faith of the Muslim partner, then he has the discretion to conduct a Muslim religious ceremony after the civil one if the couple so wish. The same applies to the other faiths, although such instances are rare if the other partner does not convert. The Catholic Church has modified considerably the demands made on a mixed-faith couple – wishing for, but no longer insisting on, the conversion of the non-Catholic partner and any children. While this has certainly made matters easier when a Catholic marries another Christian, those from other religions still feel that a religiously neutral venue is preferable. Within the Church of England there are ministers who are prepared to conduct a wedding ceremony for a mixed-faith couple, or certainly a service of blessing after a registry office marriage. In some cases they are also prepared to incorporate aspects of the non-Christian's faith. This might include certain prayers, or even marriage rituals, such as the breaking of a glass if the partner is Jewish, or wearing garlands if Sikh. The participation of a minister from the other partner's faith is sometimes permitted. Weddings with mixed-faith officiants can often involve the two ministers in much heart-searching to work out a mutually acceptable format that does not compromise their own religious integrity, although for the couples concerned such sharing is generally regarded as highly desirable so that both partners and both sets of families feel represented and involved. As Habib said: 'Seeing me married in church was difficult for some of my family, but having Muslim prayers read out by my brother standing next to the vicar made all the difference. It became our service and not just her family's.'

Those couples who were unable to obtain the wedding they wanted tended to fall into two categories. Some, like Edward, understood the rules under which ministers operated: 'I was very sad as we left the vicarage – but I knew he had to uphold the principles of the Church and I don't blame him for that.' A more common reaction, though, was frustration and bitterness, as expressed in Naomi's diatribe:

◆ I was so angry. All this garbage about how he'd love to help us but can't. Actions speak louder than words and the fact is that we got a lot of words and no action. We are going to get married come what may, it's just a matter of where, and a synagogue wedding would have meant a lot to me and an enormous amount to my parents. Instead we are being pushed towards a church ceremony or registry office. It seems terrible that the one time I really need my religion and want it to play an important part in my life, the answer is 'No'! The result is that I see no point in going back to a synagogue that has let me down and put archaic rules and regulations before real life and real people. If Judaism hasn't got time for me, well, okay, then I haven't got time for Judaism. So you can stuff all those telly-rabbis who look so friendly. When it came to it, they weren't prepared to help.

For Naomi, and many others like her from different faiths, the fact that some of their ministers may genuinely have wanted to help but had constraints on them did not alter her feeling of being badly let down. It is not just the pomp and ceremony of a religious wedding that they miss, nor is it the dashing of expectations held since childhood of one day walking down the aisle or standing under the *chuppah* (wedding canopy). It is also that, even for the religiously lapsed, they consider their wedding to be the most important day of their life and an awesome moment, and want to have an act of prayer and sense of God's blessing. It is the denial of the opportunity to have a sacred dimension that can hurt the most, and it can rankle for years afterwards. Another result is that a religious 'top of the pops' can develop with some couples approaching a variety of ministers from different faiths, shopping around to see who will be the most sympathetic and accommodating. Inevitably, comparisons are made with rabbis featuring badly because of their refusal to officiate at mixed-faith ceremonies and liberal vicars scoring high because of their willingness to marry whoever wants a church service.

Even when there is a chance of a religious ceremony, it is not necessarily taken up, either because of the conditions imposed about the faith of the children, or because one partner feels that they and their family would be so uncomfortable during the ceremony that it would be counterproductive. As Naomi went on to explain:

◆ The vicar we saw was incredibly helpful. He said he would be happy to marry us in church and could even make certain changes to the service to include some Jewish prayers. It all sounded great till he took us into the church and showed us round. My heart sank – it was so Christian! I knew I could never stand in front of a cross and my family would just freak out. I'm sure the vicar would have done a lovely service – but there was just a gut feeling that said 'Not here Naomi'. So off we went to the registrar.

When one of the partners is a Christian, some couples have found that for them the best solution is to marry in Quaker or Unitarian churches. Unlike all other denominations, they have a building that is almost entirely devoid of obviously Christian symbols, while they have a form of service that refers primarily to God rather than the Trinity. This makes the ceremony much more acceptable to the non-Christian family. Nevertheless, the vast majority of mixed-faith couples have registry office weddings. They offer a neutral venue and a civil service that pleases few but offends nobody; most people find them the least worst option. Even so, there is still the chance that some members of the family will boycott the ceremony because of their objection to the marriage in the first place. Many couples are familiar with protracted negotiations to persuade reluctant relatives to attend and the last-minute holding of breath to see who would actually turn up, who would arrive wearing black, and whether or not they walked out again in a huff. According to many couples the ceremony and the ambience of registry offices leave much to be desired, being largely a matter of form-filling and lacking any sense of occasion. 'My wedding was a bitter disappointment,' said Priscilla. 'It was an apology for a wedding. Even now, twelve years on, I'm upset when I go to church weddings and see what I missed.' Another couple expressed their disenchantment more bluntly: 'It was just ten minutes of bureaucratic pen-pushing. We could have been applying for a dog licence or paying the rates for all they cared.' While this is a common experience, it is not universal and some, like Geraldine, found that 'The registrar was so friendly and really made us feel special.' Even for the couples who enjoyed the ceremony, it was rarely their first choice and meant that religious differences had already had a major impact on their life from the very beginning of their marriage. The compromises on the wedding day are a foretaste of limitations and potential controversies in other areas in years to come.

Some couples refused to take 'no' for an answer. The deep desire for some form of spirituality has led a small but growing number to hold a Do-It-Yourself service. This is usually a short ceremony held after the registry office formalities have been completed and immediately before the reception. The service comprises of some readings from a booklet specially prepared by the couple, with prayers taken from both their traditions and supplemented by poetry and prose, religious or secular, that the couple find meaningful. Kahlil Gibran and Shakespearian sonnets are favourite material, while instrumental music – recorded or performed by friends – is also common.[1] The service is led by the couple themselves, or by a close friend or family member. Clergy are not usually involved, as the whole point of the service is to avoid the religious obstacles that they have presented, although sometimes the couple have received helpful ideas from more sympathetic ministers. Everyone present stands in a circle, and it takes place at the reception venue, be it a hotel or family garden. Those who have attended such ceremonies speak of their intimate and moving nature, while the couples often comment that, to their surprise, the task of searching for readings and selecting prayers proved a very enriching experience. These D-I-Y services may be a second best compared to what was originally desired, but they do provide an element of the sacred before the champagne and knees-up. The development of such services highlights the religious vacuum that exists for mixed-faith couples. Moreover, the attempts of those couples to fill it for themselves is a challenge to ministers of all faiths who are failing both to steer many of their flock in the direction they believe to be right, and to stay with them when they go off on a path of their own. Having been absent on the wedding day, many ministers find they are not always welcome in the rest of the couple's life.

Note

1 For a detailed description of such services and their content see Romain, Jonathan, 'Going D-I-Y: Mixed Faith Weddings' in *Common Ground*, London, Council of Christians and Jews, Numbers 3 & 4, 1992

Chapter Five

Home sweet home?

The everyday issues that mixed-faith couples
face in the kitchen, living-room and bedroom

When the fictional stage character Tevye contemplates the
marriage of his Jewish daughter to a Russian Orthodox
Christian, he exclaims: 'A fish and a bird can fall in love, but
where will they build their home?' To his mind, that sums up the
impossibility of such a union being successful. In fact many
mixed-faith couples do share the same household very happily
and have no regrets about their choice of marriage partner.
Nevertheless, they also understand what he meant, because once
the heady moments of the wedding day are over there are many
aspects of everyday domestic life that can prove problematic.

Sometimes the mixed-faith issue can start right at the front
door – quite literally in that Jews are used to having a *mezuzah*
on their front doorpost – a small tube, the size of a very short
pencil, which has a tiny scroll inside it containing excerpts from
the Bible. It is nailed onto the doorpost shortly after moving
into a new house, and then usually forgotten about, although it
is always there and is a distinctive marker, effectively declaring
the religious identity of the occupants. For Jewish couples,

however nominal, it is something that is taken for granted, and is often also placed on the doorframes of main living-rooms and bedrooms inside the house. The question of whether to have a *mezuzah* proved a contentious one for Alice and Derek, as she narrates:

◆ I was really pleased at how easy sorting out the furniture had been – what things of his we'd keep, which of mine, and then agreeing colour schemes for the new curtains. And then when he said he was going to repaint the door I said it would be nice to put up a mezuzah. He replied that just because I was Jewish, that didn't mean the house was Jewish too. I was a bit shocked and said it was nothing missionary, but that's what I was used to – my parents' and grandparents' homes had one and it was something I liked. He just looked at me and said: 'You haven't married your parents, you've married me and I don't want my front door to look like a bloody synagogue.' I never mentioned it again and told my mum that I hadn't wanted one. What else could I do?

In the case of Linda and Pete, though, there was no such friction. They had been given a decorative *mezuzah* as a present by one of Linda's cousins who did not even realize Pete was not Jewish. He thought it looked very attractive and was happy to put it up himself.

Religious symbols from other faiths can prove equally much of an issue or non-issue depending on the temperament of the other partner. Hayley was always used to a crucifix on the wall of her bedroom at home. When she went to university, she rarely attended the local church, but took a crucifix with her and put it up in her room, first in the college hall and later in lodgings. 'I'm not a great service-goer,' she explained, 'but my religion is part of me, and just knowing the crucifix is there on the wall sort of affirmed that. My husband, however, isn't Christian and said that it wouldn't feel right to have it up in the bedroom.' As a result, she keeps the crucifix in one of her clothes drawers, and every now and then opens the drawer just so as to have a look at it. She still wishes it was up on the wall. A fellow Catholic, Sonia, likes to follow her grandmother's tradition of keeping some holy water by her bedside. At first, her husband made cracks about not drinking it in the night by mistake, but he quickly stopped when he realized that while he meant it as a harmless joke, she found it very upsetting. Less easy to resolve was Maddy's feelings about Keith's Buddha. For him, it was an essential part of his faith; for her, it was akin to an idol and 'gave me the shivers'. In the end, they compromised by putting it in the spare room which was generally filled with junk, but in which he cleared a corner and created an alcove for the purposes of meditation. Nevertheless, whenever they had lots of people round for a party she always made sure that either she or Keith took their coats into the room 'in case they went in and got a shock'.

Food is often bound up with religious traditions and can necessitate preplanning of a sort not to be found in any cookbook. Ahmed does not insist that Jane buys *halal* meat, but he has asked her not to cook pork for him, and so at some breakfasts he has a cheese omelette while she enjoys bacon and eggs. Susan takes a different view, and in deference to her Jewish husband she does not have pork in the house at all, although she does relish having veal and ham pie when she is out with friends. Frank's wife goes even further, and has made an effort to master the intricacies of kosher food – such as not mixing meat and milk products in the same meal: 'Getting used to making sure that, for instance, we had fruit salad after our Sunday roast and not chocolate mousse, was a bit of a headache at first, but it came with time. I decided at the start of our marriage that if it means a lot to him, it should do to me too.' Her mother, by contrast, is less certain and is worried that she is not eating properly because of the special regulations. She might be even more concerned if she was Kate's mother, as her Muslim husband, Yaqub, tries to observe the laws of Ramadan.

This entails fasting during the day and only eating food at night throughout that month. Initially Kate objected on the grounds that he virtually never went to the mosque so it seemed ridiculous to 'suddenly get religious one month in the year, especially when it causes a lot of inconvenience for me'. The result was lengthy discussions about why Ramadan was special for Yaqub and why keeping it but ignoring other customs made sense to him even if it did not appear reasonable to her. The same could be said of many members of other faiths, whose selection of what to observe and what not to observe may seem arbitrary, or even hypocritical, to their partners, but has an internal logic for them, and relates more to the customs of their home rather than the rules of their Scriptures. In the end Kate came to understand Yaqub's perspective and a compromise was struck whereby he could eat when he liked during Ramadan, although he was responsible for providing his own meals.

For couples where one or both of the partners is used to going to their place of worship, be it intermittently or regularly, there can be difficulties. The custom that had seemed a quaint habit before marriage can turn into an annoying trait after marriage if 'time to do my own religious thing' has not been negotiated in advance. Faquir began to resent his new wife's Sunday morning visits to church, even though he had been well aware of them during their eighteen-month courtship:

◆ Somehow it didn't seem to matter at the time, but once we were man and wife, I felt, well, sort of resentful … partly because of the time she spent away, but partly because it was something I couldn't be involved in.

Much depends on whether the servicegoer takes the effort to explain exactly what happens and invites the other partner to join them if they so wish, and thus prevents them from feeling marginalized or alienated. Gail, a lapsed Jew, has been to Paul's church with him on a few occasions but generally she goes to local car boot sales while he is at Sunday morning Mass, and they both catch up with each other for a late brunch afterwards. It is also useful to know what to expect when at the other person's place of prayer. When Ashley took his Hindu wife to synagogue, it was an Orthodox one in which men and women were seated separately. The result was that they sat apart and she was in fear and trembling for the next two hours, not knowing when she was expected to sit and stand, and whether or not to do what the other women did, which in itself was confusing as some stood at times when others sat. Conversely, Michael was highly embarrassed when he went to church once with Margaret. Being Jewish he was used to not taking his wallet to the synagogue, where use of money on the Sabbath is considered wrong. He was totally flummoxed, therefore, when the collection plate came round. He had no money on him but felt he was letting down Margaret by not contributing anything.

It is not necessarily the family that prays together that stays together, but one that communicates well and respects each other's integrity. Those who are contemptuous of their partner's beliefs and traditions risk serious marital disharmony. Sometimes it can take the form of religious arrogance ('my way is the only way'); sometimes it can be in the nature of religious insult ('your faith is just based on superstition'); sometimes it is religious one-upmanship ('yours is just a higher form of idolatry'). In all cases, though, the attack on the other's faith is either a disguise for an attack on the other person, or a path that will soon lead to it. Conversely, in cases where there is discord between the couple, they sometimes prefer to blame it on each other's different religious culture rather than criticize each other directly: 'You never know where you are with Catholics, the only person they really trust is their priest', or 'Jews are tied to their families like a dog to its kennel, and they never let you go'. In doing this, they thereby shift the responsibility elsewhere and away from their own interaction.

Moreover, it is shifted onto something that cannot be altered because it is part of a larger phenomenon outside of their control. As a result, the couple avoid facing the reality of the breakdown in the relationship between the two of them, and steer away from taking any steps to remedy it.[1]

If negotiated compromises can be achieved over worship outside of the house, even greater delicacy is required for religious occasions inside the home. Even the most religiously lapsed person is caught up in some of the major 'family festivals' such as Christmas or Passover, either because of their own warm associations with the festivals or because family expectations demand that they be involved. Such times can prove to be enjoyable experiences for the other partner, a chance to share religious traditions and to meet the extended family. However, they can also be the source of problems. When Donald brought home a small Christmas tree in mid-December, he saw it as a pretty decoration for the front living-room, whereas his Muslim wife saw it as a declaration of religious war. Donald was stunned: 'She knows I never go to church; I thought she realized that for me Christmas isn't about Jesus and worshipping the Saviour, it's about family and giving presents.' After a two-hour heart-to-heart conversation his wife began to understand and consented to keep the tree, but it was typical of the assumptions that mixed-faith couples cannot take for granted about each other. Some Jewish partners can also feel very ambivalent about Christmas, celebration of which may have been portrayed by their parents as 'selling out' to Christianity when they were children. Having holly and Christmas decorations in the home can seem unnatural or even an act of betrayal, however much it is interpreted by the other partner as merely a season of goodwill without any theological overtones. 'Every year when my husband gave me a Christmas present,' said Susie, 'part of me felt it was like a bribe, egging me on to convert to Christianity. Rationally, I know that's nuts, but that's how I felt and it spoilt things.' Often the solution was a quid pro quo deal, with the house having both a Christmas tree and a menorah, the nine-branched candelabrum that is used to celebrate the festival of Hanukkah, which occurs around the same time. A Hindu-Christian couple struck a similar bargain: she could have her Diwali lamps if he could have his mistletoe.

In many cases, the person from the minority faith was already so used to receiving Christmas cards and invitations to Christmas parties from friends at work, that domestic customs presented no problems. When Charlotte asked her Jewish husband, Neil, if he minded having a Christmas tree he had no objections at all: 'To me it's no more religious than the lights in Oxford Street. And if it meant a lot to her, then why not.' Reverse tolerance does not always apply, as many Christians are unfamiliar with celebrations relating to the minority faiths. When Neil took Charlotte to his family *seder*, the religious meal at the beginning of the festival of Passover, she found herself in a room full of twenty Jewish in-laws and felt very strange: 'It was like being a lone Englishwoman abroad – silly, really, because they were all English too – and I felt an immediate kinship with the only other non-Jew there.' She also found the mixture of prayer and chatter disconcerting: 'I was used to Christian ceremonies being very solemn. Here it was serious one moment and jokes the next and I really didn't know whether to join in and risk doing so at the wrong time, or keep silent and seem stand-offish.' Her life would have been made much easier if Neil had explained what to expect beforehand.

Penelope had an even worse time in the first year of her marriage when she took round to her Jewish in-laws a gift of hot cross buns during the Passover week. She knew they had food restrictions and thought it might be appreciated. Unfortunately, it never occurred to her that hot cross buns were a Christian symbol, while flour was precisely one of the ingredients forbidden to Jews at Passover. She laughs about the incident now, but at the time she left their house in tears. For each horror story, though, there are plenty of success stories. Cherry and her Muslim husband proudly speak of their inter-faith cuisine in which they both take turns at cooking their own traditional foods – 'a mixture of Catholic and Muslim, Northumberland and Cyprus, and lots of love and laughter to give it spice.'

For Rafi the difficult times were never at annual festivals: 'We saw them coming and could plan ahead. It was the unexpected conversational points that suddenly reared up and caught us off-guard.' In mixed-faith marriages involving a Jewish partner, one such topic is Israel. For Derek it was 'just another foreign country' but for Alice it represented 'a land and a people that are very special to me'. When they watched a news item on television that was critical of Israel, Alice became very upset and said how biased was the reporting, whereas Derek could not understand why it mattered one way or the other. When he himself referred to Israel in a disparaging way, she saw it as an attack on her and a major row ensued in which the original point was forgotten and they argued instead over Alice's insistence that he was insensitive and Derek's accusation that she was neurotic. Another emotive subject for such marriages is the Holocaust and different perceptions of it. For many Christians, it was a negation of Christian values by non-Christians, while for many Jews it was an attack on Jews by Christians. 'It's not the sort of thing that crops up much,' says Rafi, 'but I sometimes wonder if Cathryn's grandfather had lived in Germany rather than in England, whether he would have joined in with the Nazis like everyone else.' For her part Cathryn is much more concerned with modern incidents of anti-Semitism which, although rare, fill her with dread:

◆ In a sense it's much harder for me as a non-Jew. Rafi was used to silly names and daubings from childhood and has learnt to laugh it off. Every time I pass a swastika on a bus-shelter it gives me the creeps. And I still have not worked out how to handle things when someone makes an anti-Jewish joke. I want to say 'How bloody

stupid' or 'Did you know I was married to a Jew?', but usually I just
go red and keep my head down.

A related issue is the question of surnames. Helena is white and
Methodist, her husband is brown and Hindu. She elected to
keep her maiden name after marriage. They tell his parents it is
because she is an only child and wants to carry on the family
surname, but the truth is that she feels an Indian surname
would lead to catty remarks and it may even reflect her own
prejudices against coloured people. Belinda was much more
forthright about her prejudices. She and her black Muslim
husband had agreed that they would both take her very
English surname: 'Just because I love him doesn't mean I love
all blacks and wanted to be associated with them. There's also
the question of the children and whether it's right to saddle
them with an obviously foreign name.' For the same reason,
another couple chose to give their children her name rather
than his, with the result that they are known as Macpherson
rather than Goldberg. Even more revealing were the comments of Tim, who admitted that he used to be inherently anti-
Semitic and that when he and his Jewish wife became engaged
'it took me a long time before I stopped worrying about
having Jewish children through her'. Fear of what might
happen to any children also affected Sabrina – a lapsed Catholic
– who had nightmares for weeks after she and her Sikh husband
had their first child: 'I kept on dreaming about race riots and
my baby being covered in blood. When I woke up I sometimes
wished I had married another white Catholic – the feeling
would only last thirty seconds, but it was enough to make me
feel thoroughly guilty.'

Mixed-faith sex is often considered a source of attraction –
the lure of the forbidden – rather than a reason for discontent,
but it can also have its problematic aspects if the partners have
conflicting attitudes to what happens in bed because of their
religious backgrounds. Camilla describes herself as a nominal

Catholic but is still strongly influenced by her upbringing, particularly the Church's teachings against contraception, even though she does not necessarily endorse them. She and her Sikh husband want to have children, but not yet, and she has no objections to the idea of family planning. However, she still feels that she does not want to be the one taking the contraceptives and so will not go on the pill, prefering her husband to wear a protective – to which he objects because he says intercourse does not feel as good when he is wearing one. The matter has now been resolved, but at one point it led to a lot of tension, culminating in a furious row, with her husband declaring: 'I'm going to bed with you, not the Pope!' Kate's problem with Yaqub related to the festival of Ramadan again. For them sex had never been just for night-time and in bed, but 'whenever the mood took us – even in the middle of breakfast'. She received a shock, therefore, when he did not respond to her daytime advances and told her that not only was food forbidden in the day during Ramadan, but also sexual relations (although they are permitted at night). 'I must admit I thought that was a bit silly,' she complained, 'but what upset me much more was that he didn't tell me beforehand or even ask if I minded. Of course, I respect his religion, but when it affects me I think I should be consulted.' Hugh felt the same about his Jewish wife. They had slept together before marriage on a few occasions and:

◆ Everything had been great in that respect. Then a month into marriage I leaned over and she said 'Not now – it's the first night of my period.' Fair enough, but then four or five days later when I thought it's all over, she tells me that the Jewish custom is to wait an extra few days after the period has stopped – resulting in twelve days abstinence in all. I blew my top and asked what the hell the point of that was. She said it was to help invigorate the marriage and some gunge about being a new bride and groom to each other each month. I told her it was the best way I knew to sink the marriage and be a new divorcee. It seemed especially ridiculous as there were tons of other Jewish laws she didn't keep. Anyway, there were floods of tears and a fairly bad patch between us. In the end we sorted it out after I had a long chat with her brother. We compromised on a week's separation, with me agreeing that I wouldn't force things if she still felt rotten the next day, while she would let me know if she finished a few days early!

In these and many other points of tension, there is often an overlap between religious teachings and cultural traditions. This is not surprising, particularly amongst minority faiths who have a strong ethnic element to family and communal life. For them, there is little distinction between specifically religious rituals and more general activities, such as eating habits, sexual mores, and family dynamics. They are all part of 'the way we do things'. It is common, therefore, for even those who do not consider themselves religious to still be strongly attached to the cultural aspects of their heritage. The problem occurs when the other partner fails to appreciate that being lapsed religiously does not mean being lapsed culturally. Jilly still finds it strange that her pork-loving Jewish husband insists on taking friends out to a Jewish restaurant because he adores the food there. Vic knows his lapsed Catholic wife has a wonderful sense of humour, but cannot understand her blind spot over jokes about the sex-life of the Pope. Atlaf keeps virtually none of the Muslim religious observances; yet has a strong Muslim identity that his Church of England wife is constantly tripping over: 'After five years of marriage, there is still an awful lot to learn. Sometimes I feel I have married a history book and I'm only halfway through it.' On one occasion she made a remark about Islam that she thought was perfectly valid but he thought was insensitive. 'But you're usually so rational,' she said, to which he replied: 'Maybe, but I'm still a rational Muslim and both parts are part of me.' This also explains why those who ignore many religious observances can still feel strongly about some that have important associations for them. When Rafi still insists on spending all day in synagogue on Yom Kippur, the Day of Atonement, his non-Jewish wife is puzzled. 'He doesn't go to synagogue at all the rest of the year, even for short services, and then he has this massive religious binge once a year. Anyway, he's an atheist so what or who on earth is he praying to?' Rafi just smiles and replies: 'True, but I'm a Jewish atheist and some things will always stay with me.' Many would regard this as hypocritical, but to those concerned it is as natural as supporting Manchester United, rarely attending any matches, but being overjoyed if they win the league championship and distraught if they do not. Being a once-a-yearer means that deep down you are still a carer and partners who misread the signals can be in for a shock. Some wish that there was a Religious Trades Description Act, so that they would have some recourse when they find that the thoroughly integrated person they thought they were marrying turned out to have a lot of cultural baggage underneath the wedding ring.

Family relationships are an important area of these cultural norms. Jilly sees her parents once a month and speaks to them two or three times on the phone in between. She regards this as normal and certainly sufficient to fulfil her Christian duty to honour her parents. She finds it highly perplexing that her Jewish husband pops in to his parents almost every other day as well as insisting that they both go there on Sunday afternoons. The fact that the phone never seems to stop going with his brothers, sisters, aunts and uncles ringing up drives her to exasperation: 'I have nothing against a single one of them – they're all lovely people – but I find this closeness pretty suffocating.' Desmond feels odd about his Jewish wife's relations for another reason:

◆ We don't see much of them, but when we do, wow, what a noise! If everyone is in a good mood, then it's hugs and jokes and backslapping; if there's an argument, it's screams and yells. There's

116

nothing in between. It's all so emotional and high-key. When we see my parents you can hear the dormouse squeak. If there is a disagreement over something, then it's a few raised eyebrows and someone goes off to take the dog for a walk. We both love our parents just as much, but boy do we do it differently!

In other instances the problem lay with the family's expectations of the husband-wife relationship. Nair tells how her Church of England husband incurred her parents' displeasure because 'he would automatically light my cigarette or open the car door for me – something that Muslim men don't do and was really frowned upon'. Family enthusiasm can sometimes be problematic. One Hindu family always brought a holy picture with them as a visiting present to their son and Presbyterian daughter-in-law. It was not intended as religious interference but simply a sign of affection. The couple felt ambivalent: 'What was a nice touch at first, soon became embarrassing. We didn't want to offend them by refusing the gifts, but if it carried on our house would look like a museum of religious art. Eventually we called a halt, my husband and I both agreed it was getting ridiculous, although I still wonder if they feel that I as the Christian put my foot down.' Visiting family from far away can be another problem. When Karnel's parents came to visit him and his new wife Barbara in the one-bedroom flat they owned, he took it for granted that he and Barbara would sleep on the couch-bed while his parents had their room. She had assumed exactly the opposite or that, even better, they would stay at a nearby bed and breakfast. 'That's what my parents would do' she said, but he felt both suggestions would be highly insulting to his parents, even though they might be more comfortable elsewhere.

The decision-making process in mixed-faith households can vary enormously. Some couples plan in advance for as many contingencies as possible; others only discuss issues when they arise. The former tends to be a much more successful method, examining topics calmly and without pressure, whereas the latter means debating in the heat of a crisis and needing to make a quick decision. Sometimes it is the wife who has the upper hand, simply because she is the one who is largely responsible for cooking or domestic rituals or the nurture of young children. As Nair said: 'I told my husband that as a Muslim I wouldn't touch pigmeat, so if he wanted pork chops he would have to cook them himself. The result is he doesn't!' However, there are two more important factors. The first is that much depends on who has the stronger personality, and that person will often get their way in religious matters, just as they do in other areas, such as choosing where to go on holiday or which house to buy. The second is that often one partner takes religious traditions more seriously than the other, and so decisions tend to be left to them, in the same way that one partner is keener on gardening or is better at doing the domestic accounts and so naturally takes charge of them. The art of compromise is a valuable skill in most marriages, but especially in mixed-faith ones. This can involve some painful choices, giving up certain habits and letting go of some expectations in return for one's partner also relinquishing some of their preconceptions. Yet it is not just a matter of the partners negating their traditions, but also, more positively, of both of them adding new dimensions to their life and permitting each other to continue those aspects of their heritage that each considers fundamental to their identity. In this respect there can be a 'learning curve' that takes some time to master. Indeed, many couples find that they experience several different stages: an initial honeymoon period, albeit punctuated by an occasional hiccup ('you never told me that'). After the euphoria has lessened, it is then followed by a period of some irritation and even hostility when differing attitudes and unfulfilled expectations simmer over into rows. Providing these difficulties are tackled sensitively, this leads to a time of readjustment and adaption, with the couple eventually becoming bicultural and agreeing what to celebrate together, what to both ignore and when to 'go off and do our own thing every now and then'. Time scales for these stages can vary enormously, varying from weeks to years, while some couples never even experience any troubles and find that 'being mixed-faith has never been a problem; we understand each other's needs and just work round them. We wouldn't have married each other if we didn't see eye to eye on everything.'

Note

1 For detailed treatment of similar ideas in cross-national marriages see Falicov, Celia Jaes, 'Cross-cultural marriages,' *Clinical Handbook of Marital Therapy*, Jacobson, Neil S. and Gurman, Alan S. (eds.), New York, Guildford Press, 1986

Chapter Six

What shall we do about the children?

The major dilemmas over how to bring up children
religiously, and how the children themselves feel about
being part of a mixed-faith household

'May all your problems be little ones' is a common remark to
newly weds, but, as any parent knows, children can be a source
of both great joy and major stress. Moreover, an enormous
amount of time can be spent worrying over a whole range of
decisions – from schools to medical matters to birthday treats –
and deciding not only what is in their best interests but how
to harmonize two sometimes divergent views on their general
upbringing. When the parents are a mixed-faith couple, the
decisions can have added complications. The couple may have
established a satisfactory way of combining two different religious backgrounds, including one partner having a faith and
the other not, although as was seen in the previous chapter
there can be several potential religious hiccups in the happiest
of marriages. Yet what might have been a good compromise,
or even a bit of a fudge, for the two of them, does not always
suffice when it comes to making decisions for a third party. The
issue is further complicated by the fact that many people who
describe themselves as lapsed find that their religious traditions

become more important to them when they have children. This is partly because they automatically turn to the church, mosque or synagogue for major cycle-of-life events such as baby blessings or initiation rites; and it is partly because they feel a deep-seated instinct to pass on to their child the traditions with which they themselves grew up, however vaguely, and even though they later veered away from them. With mixed-faith couples, the childhood experiences tend to be very dissimilar, with the memories of different stories, rituals, and smells from the kitchen wafting through their minds. Some of the parents who try to harmonize those divergences and present a joint approach for the children find it highly enriching; others find it a disaster area with unending friction, and others muddle through, knowing that they have not got it right but at least avoid major traumas. Of course, the same could be said of many parents in same-faith marriages, but while mixed-faith parents do not have a monopoly on problems with regard to children, they unquestionably have a more delicate task.

The couples that seem to manage the best are generally those who have talked over the issues before they were married and have planned ahead. In this way, they both know where the other stands, what they feel is important, where they are willing to compromise and can best avoid sudden crises or running sores. They are also better able to present a joint front to relatives who may seek to exert pressure to ensure that 'the grandchildren are brought up our way and not the other way'. The hints in such matters can start as early as the engagement with anxious relatives enquiring: 'Have you discussed what to do about the children?' Questions become more insistent once a pregnancy is announced and grandparents-to-be realize they only have nine months in which to swing any decisions their way. This can be particularly true of those who had objected to the match in the first place and who now feel that having lost the first battle they are determined to win the next round and secure the religious identity of the next generation. The welcome lull in family arguments can suddenly revive, and couples who had hoped that the bad feelings had ended are shocked to find that they had merely been simmering under the surface. Moreover, ruptures can become even deeper if grandparents-to-be, who had hoped or assumed the child would be brought up their way, are informed that that will not be the case. As Eric remarked with a mixture of sadness and anger: 'I just don't feel the same way about my non-Catholic grandson as I do about my Catholic grandson.' In other cases the pregnancy can have a more positive effect in improving relations with members of the family who had been very cool towards the couple or had even cut themselves off from all contact. Sarah's parents are Jewish, but their reaction was typical of parents from other faiths too:

◆ My father hadn't spoken to me since the wedding, being furious that I was marrying out of their faith, and although my mother also boycotted the wedding she stayed in touch through the occasional letter or phone call. When I told her I was pregnant that changed everything. She rang back an hour later and said would we like to come for tea next Sunday. The atmosphere was a bit stilted at first, and there are still subjects we avoid, but now, four months later, we're really quite close again. It's wonderful. When I asked my mother why my father had made such a turnaround she said she had told him 'Look, we've lost a daughter and it's got us nowhere. I'm not going to lose a grandchild too. And there wasn't much he could say to that.'

Amongst the many decisions that parents have to make are the very immediate ones of what to do about initiation rites when the baby is born. If one of the parents is Christian, a christening may be expected; if the baby is male and one parent is Jewish or Muslim, then circumcision is the norm, for Jews on the eighth day after birth, for Muslims by thirteen years old but

122

increasingly performed at an early age. The potential for friction between partners who have not discussed the issue beforehand is enormous. The 'we will cross that bridge when we come to it' brigade often find that they do not reach the other side but fall off. Pam's joy at giving birth was shattered when her Muslim husband said he would ring both sets of parents and then contact the doctor about a circumcision. 'I felt horrified: our son was only a few minutes old and Rashid wanted to start cutting him up; it seemed barbaric.' Janice faced the opposite problem; being Jewish she assumed their new son would be circumcised and was appalled that her husband said it was out of the question. In both cases, and many others like them, the birth that should have been a joyous event proved to be a major upset. For those whose traditions take circumcision for granted it seems a perfectly natural family tradition which also has some health arguments in its favour; for those unused to circumcision, it is a form of mutilation on a defenceless child that is to be resisted strenuously. The fact that Jesus was circumcised on the eighth day – which is why 1 January is known as the Feast of the Circumcision in the Church calendar – tends to carry little weight for Christians who are worried by the notion.[1] Male parents feel personally involved in another way: those who are not circumcised see the child's circumcision in terms of how they themselves would feel if they were about to be circumcised (forgetting that a newly born child has a nervous system that is not fully developed and does not feel anything like the amount of pain an adult would); they may also have nightmares about emasculating their own sexual prowess. Those who are circumcised have a strong desire for the child to 'look like me, so that when we go to the loo together we are the same'. It is to avoid such emotive debates that a high percentage of mixed-faith couples 'pray that we have a girl'.

Some parents agree to a quid pro quo arrangement: a baby blessing in both places of worship, either attended by both sets of families or each one going to that of their own tradition. Not all swops are equal, though, as one couple found out after having their son both circumcised and baptized in what they thought left him part of both traditions. In fact, circumcision by itself does not make one Jewish (or Muslim), whereas baptism does label that person a Christian. In this respect, baby blessings are the most innocuous ceremonies, involving nothing physical, nor irrevocably committing the child to one particular camp. Those looking for a ceremony that includes everyone and compromises no one sometimes find them an ideal solution, although much depends on the attitude of the minister and how much they are prepared to tailor the service to the couple's needs. Unlike the marriage service, there are no legal or even internal regulations concerning such blessings, and ministers of all faiths have much discretion over the ceremony. This applies also to the venue, which can be in their place of worship or in the couple's home, or at some other location.

For all couples, even those who decide not to have any religious ceremony at all, there is still the unavoidable question of the child's name. Different religious and cultural traditions can surface in unexpected ways: Kerry, a Methodist, thought it would be proper to call their first-born son after her father, who had just celebrated his 70th birthday, as a token of respect for him. Her husband had no objections either to the name or to his father-in-law, but felt that their son should be named after his father who had died five years earlier, in keeping with the Jewish tradition of naming a child after a relative who had died rather than one still alive. Being Catholic, Maria felt it important that her first child carried the name of a saint, and proposed the name John, whereas her atheist husband wanted no such associations and preferred a 'non-denominational' name such as Roy. The significance of names also affected Shahid and Judy. Shortly after they married, her sister, Tina, died of cancer at a very young age. After the church service, Judy suggested that if they had a daughter, they would name her after Tina, to which Shahid readily agreed, having already assumed that they would not give their children a Hindu name. However, when he realized that Tina was short for Christine, he felt very ambivalent about such an obviously religious name being given to his daughter and also nervous about how his family would react. The problem was not unique to them. A Muslim father was content with his lapsed C. of E. wife's suggestion of Natalie as a name for a possible girl, until he noticed in a name book that it actually meant 'child of Christmas', something she had not realized either. A Catholic wife wanted to name her daughter Teresa, but her Protestant husband objected because 'in the circles I mix in, it would stand out like a sore thumb, telling the world "this kid is Catholic".' Ethnic names also act as instant labels. The solution for many couples is to choose relatively neutral names, particularly modern ones that have no religious association, such as Gary or Tracy, or those from the Bible that are common to the Judeo-Christian heritage, such as Daniel or Sarah. Middle names are often used to include more conspicuous names in a way that will placate relatives but not lead to catcalls in the school playground. It is for couples such as these that in the Jewish world a baby-naming book with a special chapter for mixed-faith families has recently been produced.[2] Commercial instincts have recognized a ready market and are reflecting social needs much more astutely than many religious institutions.

The decision about names is something that at least only needs to be tackled once per child. The religious upbringing that they receive is a much longer process that can last for almost two decades. Two separate issues are involved, which are often confused but which couples find much more helpful if they keep separate. One is the religious identity of children. This is the way in which they perceive themselves, and also how others label them. It is the response given to questions they will meet in all walks in life, ranging from nursery school friends who say 'I'm Christian. What are you?', to forms to be filled out if they enter hospital and the box that says 'Religion of patient'. The second aspect is their religious education. This is the religious knowledge that they acquire, whether picked up from parents and other relatives; or taught at religion school. The distinction between the two is crucial, because the former is a matter of what children believe in, while the latter is what they know about. Moreover the two need not necessarily be the same, and children can be brought up identifying with one faith yet exposed to the traditions of other faiths. This can be particulary important for mixed-faith families where flexibility and openness can be essential requirements for their religious policy vis-à-vis the children. As a result there are several different options that are available to parents, depending on what they feel is the best course of action. Each one has its own advantages and disadvantages:

1 *Children having a single religious identity, with religious education in that faith only.* This enables the children to know exactly where they stand and gives them a firm sense of direction. However, unless there is enormous sensitivity to the partner whose faith is not being followed, he/she may feel marginalized and cut off from the children, while that person's family may also feel estranged.

2 *Children having a single religious identity, but with religious education in both faiths.* This allows the children to know who they are religiously, yet be heir to the traditions of both parents. A possible problem is that it can puzzle those children who are given one identity yet decide they prefer the other faith.

3 *Children having a dual religious identity, with religious education in both faiths.* This results in the children sharing fully both traditions, but while some children accept a dual identity as natural, it can confuse those who want to know 'but which one am I *really*?'

4 *Children having a joint religious identity, with religious education in the syncretized faith.* This treats the two faiths as one and mixes together the customs and values. This can lessen potential tensions, although it can blur important distinctions and degenerate into a few annual feasts without any coherent system of beliefs.

5 *Children having the religious identity of a third faith, which is different from that into which the parents were each born but which they have decided to adopt for the family as a whole as a neutral compromise.* This only applies when both partners feel the need for a spiritual life and are also prepared to leave their own faith. It generally involves change to one that has a common denominator e.g. a Catholic and a Baptist becoming Unitarian, or a Muslim and a Jew becoming Bahai. It may solve many problems, although it depends on both partners being content with the new faith, while it can leave both sets of grandparents confused.

6 *Children having no religious identity, but with religious education in both faiths.* This permits the children to make a choice for themselves when they reach an age of maturity. However, this can cause the problem of them feeling guilty that if they choose the faith of one parent they may seem to be rejecting the other parent, even if that is not the case at all. The 'rejected' parent may also feel hurt.

7 *Children having no religious identity, and no religious education.* This is an alternative attempt at being neutral, with children making their own decisions in adulthood un-encumbered by parental influences. However, one cannot choose from a vacuum and so the result tends to be no choice at all and an absence of religion in later life.

In each case, the success of the policy depends on how well the couple have planned ahead. This includes sensitivity to each other, both their own observances and their latent religious loyalties. Leslie did not practise his Judaism and was happy for his wife to send them to church Sunday school, but was very upset when they came home and told him that Jews were not as good as Christians. Laura, a lapsed Catholic, had agreed that her children could be brought up Muslim, but was very embarrassed when she found that her eleven-year-old son thought the Eucharist was a pop group (obviously confusing it with the real group, the Eurythmics) and just laughed out aloud when he was told that Madonna was in the New Testament. Laura regretted how little they knew about traditions which, although she had given them up, were still embedded in her consciousness. Sensitivity was needed also with regard to each other's family. In a household, for instance, in which the children are being brought up Muslim, are they allowed to visit the mother's parents and enjoy Christmas lunch and have presents? Is it dangerous religious indoctrination or just fun family gathering if children brought up Sikh attend their Jewish grandparents and enjoy the Passover meal? Ultimately there is no right or wrong approach, but whatever is appropriate for each particular couple. If there is one golden rule it is that they act in harmony. Children will often accept the way in which they are brought up providing it is consistent and genuinely believed in by both parents. Ten-year-old William takes it as natural that he is a Buddhist Jew, because one parent is Buddhist and one Jewish and they treat both as the family faith. It was something of a shock to him when he first realized that not everyone else in the world was a Buddhist Jew and he considers friends with just one faith as 'a bit odd really, like having only one hand if you're used to having two.' Dual identity makes sense to him because it comes over strongly at home and it feels normal. Conversely, children are very good at spotting hypocrisy, inconsistencies or rifts between the parents. Parents who have given inadequate attention to religious upbringing, or who have disagreements between themselves, usually communicate their doubts to the children and only succeed in passing on confused attitudes. The result is indifference, or even outright hostility, to religion. Another consequence is the effect of children on the parents themselves. Melinda and her husband had decided not to have any religious celebrations in the house, although they would attend services or attend family festivities. By the time her son was five, she became very agitated that there was no Christmas tree for him at home: 'I knew how much it had meant to me as a child and I felt he was being deprived of something special.' Her reluctance to broach the subject with her husband was partly because of the agreement they had made, but also because she was worried what religious concessions he might demand in return.

In addition to the emotional energy involved in religious education, several of the above policies demand much hard work. Because society at large tends to live in an 'either/or' mental framework which assumes that children have to be one religion or the other, it takes effort to maintain a dual identity or dual education. It is not only a matter of mastering the facts, but also of keeping a genuine balance in the home. This is compounded by the differences between the couple – one of whom may feel more strongly about their faith than the other, while one may spend more time with the children, and one may be better at dealing with religious topics with them. Outside influences also have to be taken into account, such as the mass marketing of Christmas in the high street or the religious nature of school assemblies. Those who are atheist and do not wish their children to be 'religiously bullied' often find themselves fighting wider currents that take for granted at least some religious identity. The Scout and Guide oath to 'do my duty to God and the Queen' may seem innocent to many, but doctrinaire to secularists. Some of the more committed parents have banded together to form interfaith religion schools that meet on a Sunday, weekly or fortnightly, in someone's home and have drawn up interfaith curricula. Others have formed groups that concentrate on one faith, but which acknowledge and accept the mixed-faith background from which the children come and take account of it in the lessons.[3] Many couples report that the good intentions with which they started – home celebrations, religious stories and visits to different places of worship – gradually wilted under all the other pressures that parents face, from appointments at the dentist to supervising homework to watching football matches to hunting for lost guinea pigs. Somewhere along the way, God got lost too, and only reappeared for Christmas and similar major events in the other faiths.

A radically different course of action that is adopted by a limited number of parents highlights some interesting lessons. They have chosen to give different religious identities to different children. Kevin is Jewish and his wife Isabel is a Quaker. Their children were brought up in their own image, with Daniel being Jewish, going to synagogue with his father and attending synagogue religion school, while his sister Virginia is a Quaker and went with her mother to meetings of the Society of Friends. The arrangement would seem to be a recipe for religious schizophrenia, or at least for a very divided household, but in fact has worked well. The children, now in their twenties, have a well-balanced attitude to religion, report no memories of conflict in their childhood or any disquiet now, and have maintained the separate identities in which they were brought up respectively. No doubt a similar arrangement with a different set of parents might not have worked so well, but the case illustrates how what to the outsider may appear highly peculiar can seem perfectly satisfactory to those in the situation. It also demonstrates how the key to success is not always the policy itself but the effort and sensitivity that is put into it. A similar division of children is also found in some Catholic-Protestant marriages, with children being baptized alternatively in Catholic and Protestant churches and being brought up in the different identities. To non-Christians this may seem a small divide, but those within the Church still find it a large gulf, while families living in Northern Ireland are well aware of the tribal rivalries between members of the two groups. Splitting the children religiously was in fact part of state law in Hungary prior to the First World War. Parents in a mixed-faith marriage could determine the religious identity of their children, but if they failed to do so, sons followed the faith of the father and daughters that of the mother.

The success or failure of parents' efforts with their children is not always in their hands alone. The extended family can play a helpful role, sharing their religious traditions and insights; alternatively, they can create problems through a variety of means, such as by excluding them or by interfering with them or by denigrating them in front of the children. Important, too, is the reaction of the religious bodies. Marcia was baptized a Catholic, but had very little involvement and was married in a registry office to her non-Catholic husband. When her children were of school age, she decided it was time to give them a religious direction and, with the consent of her husband, approached the local Catholic priest:

◆ I was horrified. He had the gall to tell me that in the eyes of the Church our marriage was not considered religiously valid. Didn't the last ten years count for anything? Did he really expect me to entrust my children to his care when he didn't even recognize our relationship? There was no way I was going to have our marriage denied or expose the children to an institution with such antiquated teachings. With one sentence he lost me and my children forever.

Miriam tells how she walked out of synagogue life when she went to enter her children at religion school and was told she would be put on the membership form as 'Miss …' because the Orthodox law did not recognize the existence of her non-Jewish husband. By contrast, other couples record how a sympathetic and sensitive response could make all the difference: 'The minister stuck his hand out and said, "I am so glad *both* of you came" and we knew we and the children would feel at home.' At another set of parents' first approach, Gordon, the non-Jewish partner, was immediately put at ease when 'The rabbi joked to me, "Did you have to drag her here kicking and screaming?" It broke the ice and we enrolled the kids soon after.'

The problems of religious education can apply equally to children of same-faith parents. They too can suffer from poor or inconsistent upbringing. As yet there are no statistics on the relative success of respective situations, although some work has been done in the United States. A survey of Christian-Jewish marriages traced the membership of both the parents and their children:[4]

	Mixed-faith parents	Children of mixed-faith parents
Church	36%	21%
Synagogue	9%	3%
Both	6%	–
Neither	49%	76%

The results indicate that virtually half the parents have no membership, which suggests that their children are unlikely to have much religious upbringing. Amongst those parents who are members, there is a significant drop in the religious affiliation of their children, whether attached to church, synagogue or both. The only category showing a marked increase is that of those who drop out of any formal religious association. It suggests that while some parents may be able to pass on a strong religious heritage – single or dual – to their children, a considerable percentage failed to do so. The study also examined the celebration of festivals:

	Teenage children of mixed-faith marriages	Adult children of mixed-faith marriages
Christmas	95%	95%
Easter	80%	53%
Passover	37%	35%
Yom Kippur	20%	18%

These figures provide two lessons: first, that Jewish customs are observed less than those of the majority culture, Christianity; second, that those celebrations which take place largely in the home (Christmas and Passover) are kept more than those which are church or synagogue based (Easter and Yom Kippur), while their drop-off rate is less as those children become adults and run their own homes.

Dropping out of religion is not the only reaction of children of mixed-faith families. A smaller number drop into religion. Having had either no religious input at all, or some that left them dissatisfied, they yearn for a spiritual approach that will answer inner needs. As a result they may try to educate themselves religiously and seek out mainstream religious institutions. It is also possible they will be attracted to more intense forms of religion – whether fervent evangelical Christianity, ultra-Orthodox Judaism, or extreme Muslim sects. Some will also find cults appealing – which offer both the religious certainty and emotional pull that had been lacking in their childhood. It can also be a form of rebellion. Just as some children hurt their parents by rejecting their God, so others gain revenge by taking up the God that their parents had abandoned.

It is all too easy to chronicle where mixed-faith parents make mistakes in the religious education of their children. If there are any certain ways of doing it right and with positive results, they would seem to include the following:

- each partner to have a clear idea of what is important religiously to themselves
- share this with each other, as well as their likes and dislikes of the other's religious background
- have a plan of action that is developed well in advance, preferably before marriage
- check that both partners feel comfortable with the plan, both what is included and what is excluded
- inform the immediate relatives in the two families, so that they too are prepared in advance, and can voice any opinions before the children arrive
- where possible incorporate the family to help with the informal education (such as home ceremonies and festive meals) both so as to use their experience and so as to make them feel valued and part of the process
- be prepared to change the plan as circumstances demand and to take into account events and personal feelings which had not been foreseen
- be honest with the children about both one's beliefs and one's doubts, about both the points of agreement and disagreement between each other, and about the prejudices they may meet elsewhere
- be willing to use ministers, friends, or relatives whom the parents respect as resource people or even role models
- make religion something that permeates the house (be it through food, books, conversations, or night-time prayer) and is a regular experience rather than just an occasional issue or one that only exists outside the home
- help the children to express their feelings, doubts and beliefs and encourage them to ask questions freely
- allow them to be different from the parents if they so choose, and without feeling guilty

But how does being born into a mixed-faith family feel from the children's point of view? Some, like Lewis, remember a religious haze that was 'very confusing; I never knew what I was supposed to believe in. In the end I just decided that religion wasn't for me, and it plays no part in my life now.' Others, such as Lynne, are much more resentful of their lack of identity: 'My parents left me stranded religiously and I always felt deprived compared to other kids. To a certain extent it has affected my relationships with other people in that I'm always hankering after something I can't quite define.' The sense of having missed out on something that might have been meaningful was a theme echoed by many. Equally problematic were those who became a battleground in the religious war between their parents: 'For me, religion meant rows. I remember Mum lit some candles one night and Dad yelled she'd burn the house down and insisted she put them out. When I read somewhere about religion being about loving your neighbour as yourself I laughed and thought – not in our place!' Several recall conflicts with other members of the family. 'We only ever saw one set of grandparents. Apparently father's parents wouldn't meet us because he married my mother. I heard him arguing with them on the phone once and remember thinking how unpleasant they must be.' Some felt the greatest hurt was when they were rejected by representatives of the religion to which they thought they belonged:

◆ My father was Jewish and proud of his roots while my mother was nothing really, the daughter of a very lapsed Catholic – so Dad took charge religiously and I was brought up more Jewish than anything else and I certainly thought of myself as Jewish and sometimes we went to synagogue together. But when I went to college and turned up in the local synagogue by myself, the rabbi said that as my mother was not Jewish, nor was I, although I was welcome to attend as a Christian. I was stunned: I wasn't a Christian, and for him to tell me I wasn't Jewish felt awful. It was like being told I wasn't human. If I wasn't Jewish, then everything up till then had been based on falsehood.

Another child of a Jewish father and non-Jewish mother, whose personal identity as a Jew was not matched by his official non-Jewish status, was even more bitter: 'If I'd been caught by Hitler he would have considered me Jewish enough to be sent to the gas chambers, but my birth wasn't sufficient for the Orthodox rabbi'.[5] A variant of this difference between their self-perception and the view of the outside world was that several who had a Christian identity were judged in terms of the other parent's religious background. Oliver goes to church regularly once a month, as he has done since childhood, but many consider him Jewish because he carries his father's surname, Weinstock. Even fellow congregants think of him as a Jewish Christian and he has reluctantly accepted that he will always be labelled as different. Others in a similar position remember being beaten up at school because they were thought of as Jewish even though they knew they were not. 'It was the worst of both worlds', recalls Francis. 'I suffered from anti-Semitism but hadn't even got a sense of pride in my roots with which to combat it.' For some children, this led them to be angry at their Jewish, or other minority, faith father for giving them a label that landed them in trouble. More wilful children admit that they used the religious differences between their parents to their own advantage. Glen remembers telling his Muslim father he would join the Ramadan fast if he did not have to go to rehearsals for the school Christmas carol concert – which his mother was very keen on but he loathed doing – as the extra long day made him too exhausted. Some who were being brought up with a dual identity inadvertently hurt one parent by expressing a preference for the other parent's faith, as did Gayatri, child of a Hindu-Catholic household, who told her father that she liked Jesus better than Krishna because she received better presents on his birthday.[6] Mat had happy childhood experiences in a dual upbringing, but they were clouded in later life when he formally adopted his father's religion and knew his mother felt let down. By contrast, there were other children who reacted neither by preferring one faith to another, nor by dropping religion altogether, but by seeking their own path elsewhere. As one put it: 'I'm Jewish by birth, Christian by upbringing and Buddhist by choice.'

If there are plenty of children who think of the pitfalls their parents fell into, there are also many who record a much happier experience: 'My parents made an effort to do lots of fun things at the festivals – special foods, dressing up, visiting relatives, singing and dancing – and we really had the best of both worlds and thought life for those who only had one religion must be rather boring.' Aza agrees: 'The most important lesson I learnt from sharing my parents' two faiths was tolerance, tolerance of other people's differences. It was a religious principle that has stood me in good stead in all walks of life.' Ruby had no identity problems with her mixed heritage and told of the adapted ditty she made up as an eight-year-old: 'Roses are red, violets are blueish, Daddy is Methodist and we are Jewish.' Karl found his double faith made sense:

◆ As a child, I knew that there were lots of religions and that I belonged to two of them, and that if I had different parents it might have been another two – but it didn't matter as we were all the children of God. In fact my mother taught me all the different names people used – Yahweh, Jesus, Allah, Krishna and so on – but we knew which were our special names for God and felt comfortable with that.

For children like Karl and other 'success stories', having mixed-faith parents meant enriching their experiences and broadening their horizons. As might be expected, they often see no objection to themselves entering a mixed-faith marriage. Conversely, those who felt they suffered from the experience will express a preference for a same-faith marriage 'because it will give greater stability and direction'. However, a significant number of the latter will so lack any religious identity that they do not feel they belong to any religious group strongly enough to justify a conscious decision to marry into them.

Another dimension to the issue of children, which seems to reinforce the problems popularly associated with their religious education, is evidence that mixed-faith parents have fewer children than do same-faith parents. A study in Sheffield in 1974 revealed that same-faith Jewish couples had an average birth rate of 1.89 children, with 23% having no children at all, while mixed-faith couples had an average birth rate of 0.75 children, with 75% having no children at all.[7] This reflects similar research elsewhere, which also shows a lower birth rate and a higher incidence of childlessness.[8]

Two main explanations present themselves. One is that many mixed-faith couples decide to avoid the potential problems involved in raising children by electing to be childless. This is confirmed by couples such as Colin and Marilyn, now in their sixties, who felt that the general social climate was so unconducive to mixed-faith children that 'it was fairer not to have any'. This may apply less for today's mixed-faith children, although the potential turmoils the two parents might face still remain. The second reason is that in marriages which hope to produce children there is a greater likelihood that one partner will convert to the religion of the other, whether to harmonize the family faith or to pacify enraged families. In second or late marriages, in which children are not expected, conversion can often lose its relevance, and so increases the number of childless mixed-faith couples that appear in the statistics.

Notes

1 Luke 2:21
2 Diamant, Anita, *The New Jewish Baby Book*, Woodstock, Vermont, Jewish Lights Publishing, 1993
3 For a more detailed account of these classes, see Tenner, Debi, 'Interfaith Sunday School Lessons' in *Dovetail*, Missouri, February/March 1994, p.8 and June/July 1994, p.10; Memel,

David, 'What shall we teach the children?' in *Netnews*, London, 1993, p. 3

4 Mayer, Egon, *Children of Intermarriage: A Study in Patterns of Identification and Family Life,* New York, American Jewish Committee, 1983

5 According to the infamous Nuremberg Laws issued by the Nazis in 1935, which deprived Jews in Germany of citizenship and most civil rights, a Jew was defined as anyone with one Jewish grandparent

6 For details of this family's attempt to make the two traditions co-exist in the same household, see Gajiwala, Astrid, 'The spirit of dialogue' in *The Month*, London, March 1995, p. 93. See also *The Month*, August 1990

7 Kosmin, Barry, Bauer, Marzy and Grizzard, Nigel, *Steel City Jews*, London, Board of Deputies of British Jews, 1976, p. 18

8 For details of studies in Germany and the United States, see Berman, Louis A. *Jews and Intermarriage, A Study in Personality and Culture,* New York, Joseloff, 1968, p. 231

Chapter Seven

Is parting such sweet sorrow?

What happens later on in life when people change,
or when marriages fail, or when death parts
mixed-faith couples

'Marriage is not a word, it's a sentence' declared Mae West. Whether one agrees entirely with her or not, it is certainly true that marriages can last a long time, and often covering a period during which one or both partners can change considerably in terms of their needs and interests. This applies to religious matters too, and can mean that their attitude to religion at the time of the wedding can be very different fifteen years later. Holly found this out to her cost: 'I thought I had married a lapsed Muslim who didn't care two hoots about God, and he then suddenly gets religious and wants me to convert and come to the mosque with him.' In Joy's case, it was she who reverted to her roots:

◆ Judaism didn't mean anything to me and I was quite happy to marry Bert in church, and when the children were born I had them both baptized. But then I started to think about being Jewish – there was no problem with the marriage and we were all very happy together – it was just something deep inside me – and I read Jewish books and went to synagogue; it was a bit daunting after so long away, but I felt I was coming home. In the end I started taking the children with me – Bert didn't mind – and now the older one thinks of himself as Jewish too.

Joy was fortunate in having a tolerant husband. Other spouses feel angry that the person they thought they were marrying was turning out to be different. Neither Chandana nor her Sikh husband were attached to their respective faiths and agreed to have a 'religion-free home'. But eleven years later she began to observe some Hindu festivals, doing so privately in order not to upset the marital applecart. Nevertheless, he was very upset when he found out, feeling threatened by it and accused her of letting down her side of the bargain.

The reawakening of religious urges can be related to external events, be they positive or negative – such as the birth of children or the death of a parent. Sometimes they can reflect difficulties within the marriage, but not necessarily so. They can also be due to the passage of time and gradual changes in one's priorities and identity. This is particularly the case as many people marry in their twenties at a time when they are most distant emotionally from their religious roots and faith-community, but from then onwards, many begin a slow, almost imperceptible journey back towards their childhood upbringing. In a mixed-faith marriage this can mean the partners going in very different directions. While some will share each other's experiences and support their quest, others will react with resentment and hostility. In yet other families, the opposite process can occur, whereby one partner who seemed to accept or even welcome the different faith of the other partner, then sets out to change it. Josh, for instance, was a lapsed Jew who was attracted to Rosemary and married her despite his parent's opposition to having a Christian daughter-in-law, claiming that he was not bothered in the slightest. However, once married, he tried to mould her into being a

141

good Jewish wife. It was not that he had deliberately hidden his true intentions when courting her. For him and many others like him, it was because subconsciously he was much more at home in his own faith than he realized. Having proved his independence from his parents by marrying her, or having exorcized the adventurous streak in him, he now wanted to return to the religious and cultural pattern with which he was familiar. As it happened, Rosemary was happy to fit in with his wishes, but others can feel deceived and very angry at the apparent volte-face.

Not all marriages survive and the breakdowns can be painful. When mixed-faith marriages end in divorce, there can be added complications to the emotional upheavals. One is that much of the resentment that may be felt towards the ex-spouse can be given a religious tinge, in which all the latter's co-religionists are judged in his/her light. Amanda had an acrimonious end to her marriage, and as well as listing her Muslim husband's many faults, she declared: 'I started off admiring Islam, now I despise it.' Micky spoke with equal passion when he said: 'Nothing converts a tolerant Gentile into an anti-Semite as quickly as getting divorced from a Jew.' Others, of course, can separate their dislike for one particular person and the rest of his faith-community, but it is not so easy to keep a balance when children are involved. When Hakim and Joanne split up they had two young children whom they had brought up Muslim. Now, however, Joanne had sole custody and control, while she herself found solace in the church and began to take the children to services there. It was confusing for them, while Hakim was furious but helpless. Rita faced a different problem when she became divorced. She and her Hindu ex-husband had joint care of their son, who lived with her most of the time, and they agreed that neither would take him to any form of religious worship. Two years later, she remarried, this time to an observant Jew, and it seemed natural that all three of them should go to synagogue together. Her ex-husband was adamant that the original agreement be maintained, leaving Rita disappointed and their son feeling annoyed that he was having no say in the matter. A further dimension is that a large number of children of divorced couples spend midweek with one parent and all or part of weekends with the other parent. This can mean that they are constantly chopping and changing their religious orientation – be it between two different faiths or between one faith and the absence of a faith – and although this can happen within a mixed-faith marriage too, it is even more destabilizing if accompanied by derogatory remarks about the ex-partners and their faith. Sometimes the abuse can be visited on the children, as happened to Dinah, whose non-Jewish mother once shouted at her: 'Get out of my kitchen, you dirty little Jew.' Moreover, as many religious services take place over the weekends, it shifts the balance of religious celebration in favour of the 'weekend parent' and that can also lead to friction between the former partners.

The question must be asked as to whether mixed-faith marriages are more likely to experience a divorce than same-faith marriages? Statistical evidence has provided mixed results. Several different research projects have been undertaken, although largely limited to very particular locations, and the conclusion of most is that mixed-faith couples have a marginally higher rate of divorce than same-faith couples, but the difference is so slight as to be inconclusive.[1] Some other studies aver that mixed-faith marriages are definitely more prone to instability, with the divorce-rate being several times higher.[2] Whilst the social scientists are arguing the exact percentages, there are some clear reasons why the findings should point to a more negative result. One is the pressure that a mixed-faith marriage can face because of the extra compromises and difficult decisions ahead of them. This is magnified if the surrounding families add to the conflict and actively foster dissension between the couple. A second is that a person who is prepared to flout their parents' wishes in the choice of marriage partner may also be more liable to resist the compromises necessary for a harmonious relationship. A third is that a basic human need is security, and if one's marriage partner is often presenting challenges – be it in terms of emotional expectations, or family roles, or ways of communicating – this can be unsettling and lead to a collapse of trust. A fourth possible reason applies to those who intermarry specifically as an act of rebellion against their family or community, and whose relationship is based on feelings against others rather than for that partner, in which case it may well end in disarray. A fifth reason is that if a marriage has taken place in the face of parental opposition, then relatives are less likely to rally round in times of trouble and offer the support that is often crucial in sustaining otherwise reasonably successful marriages through a difficult period. A sixth factor is that, as a generalization, the more religiously observant a couple the less likely they are to divorce – because marriage is seen not only as a bond between two people, but as a sacrament or a union made before God, with an aura of sanctity that encourages them to persevere through difficulties; as mixed-faith marriages often, though not always, involve people without such a perspective and the wedding is usually conducted without a religious ceremony, it is inevitable that resistance to divorce will be lower amongst their ranks. A breakdown of the figures from one study revealed:[3]

Divorce rate for Catholic couples	11.2%
Divorce rate for Jewish couples	17.6%
Divorce rate for Catholic/non-Catholic couples	28.9%
Divorce rate for Jewish/non-Jewish couples	41.0%

Despite the six possible reasons for divorce specifically among mixed-faith partners, interviews with such couples often elicit the comment that it was not religious differences that caused the breakup but a range of other, unrelated aspects. These include incompatibility of lifestyles, growing apart emotionally, financial crises, sexual problems. In some cases, these were enough to lead to the separation; in other cases, religious differences did play a role in that all the other tensions meant that the initial tolerance and goodwill that had minimized any religious flashpoints evaporated, and previous hiccups now became major conflicts. As Hilary explained: 'There were so many things fundamentally wrong with the marriage that it was doomed to fail; when we hit religious issues as well, that was the last straw that broke an already fragile camel's back.' Sometimes religion was used to cover up the other problems: fierce battles were fought over domestic rituals or children's religious education that were really expressions of the underlying struggle between the two spouses which they either did not recognize or were unwilling to confront. In essence, one of the prime causes of divorce is marriage, and same-faith marriages have shown that they are not immune to discord. Nevertheless, there is probably some sense in words of the modern Hebrew poet Yehuda Amichai:

> Advice for good love:
> Don't love a woman from far away.
> Choose one from nearby the way a sensible house
>   will choose local stones that have frozen in the
>   cold and basked in the same scalding sun

It is undoubtedly easier to marry someone who shares the same religious and cultural background, behavioural patterns and expectations. Mixed-faith marriages can require an extra degree of sensitivity and tolerance to make them work. As the anthropologist Margaret Mead put it: 'If you are not going to marry the boy next door – and if you do, you may die of boredom – then you are going to have to work much harder.'

Of course, there are many mixed-faith marriages that last a long time and are blissfully happy. Many of those couples would reverse the sentiment expressed by Margaret Mead. In their view, their marriage is successful precisely because it is a mixed-faith marriage and therefore involved much effort in the early stages of the relationship. Desmond summed up the feelings of many when he said:

◆ Unlike most other couples who just worry about the wedding day, we really had to plan in advance – home life, children, what to do over Christmas, how often family would visit, when we needed to give each other space and so on. It was a big agenda, but we really got to know each other on a much deeper level and it was enormously helpful, like mapping out the course of our married life so that we knew exactly what we were committing ourselves to. And it wasn't just the two of us, but involved other people too – family, friends, a local minister – and although we didn't always take everybody's advice, it was good to have it as background information. Over the years, we've made a few changes here and there, but by and large we've stuck to that plan and it's stood us in good stead.

In effect, it means that many mixed-faith couples undergo a form of marriage guidance in advance. They are more knowledgeable about each other; they are more prepared for the issues that confront all couples; and they have learnt to negotiate with each other in areas of difference between the two of them. Clearly, this does not apply to all mixed-faith marriages, and those that fail to look further ahead than the wedding dress are more likely to encounter problems.

There are also many couples whose mixed-faith marriage is their second and follows a divorce from a same-faith partner. Several of them have commented that not only is it a better match emotionally, but, paradoxically, it is more successful religiously too. Irene found that she faced terrible traumas with her first husband – a fellow Jew – over keeping home observances and giving the children a Jewish education, all of which he was opposed to and sought to obstruct as much as possible.

'It was as if I had married out,' she declared, 'and came as a devastating shock.' In her subsequent marriage, her Catholic husband proved very supportive and encouraged her to celebrate her own faith fully. Alf was equally dismissive of his first wife, whom he had met through the Christian Union at university:

◆ One day she walked out on me without warning and left behind two children under five. Not very Christian behaviour. I've remarried a Hindu girl and she not only keeps the Ten Commandments, but teaches them to my children. Who would you say is the better person – the Christian who betrayed me and the children, or the non-believer who picked up the pieces?

Naturally, these cases reflect more about the character of the first partners than they do about the wisdom of same-faith marriages, but the numerous testimonies along the same theme indicate that assumptions about same-faith marriages being automatically better than mixed-faith ones must be challenged.

Those whose mixed-faith life together is not ended prematurely by divorce face added questions as they approach death. One is what sort of ceremony the partners wish to have. Some religious cemeteries have bye-laws restricting them, or plots within them, to members of that particular faith. It may mean, for instance, that if a husband dies first and is buried in a Jewish cemetery, his Christian widow may not be able to be buried there when she is laid to rest. This can prove highly upsetting if the couple have not investigated the matter beforehand. Edith's story is typical in this respect:

◆ When my husband died I never thought to ask about what would happen to me. So it was an awful shock to find I couldn't be buried next to him. I know that when we are dead it won't really matter, but I had always imagined lying side by side, and now I will be plonked somewhere else. It's very distressing really.

The hurt can also be felt by the children when they have to visit their parents in separate sections, or even separate cemeteries, and not have the comfort of knowing that they are together in death as they were in life. Most civic cemeteries do have areas that are open to anyone irrespective of their religion or lack of religion, in which case the couple can be together, although this may not satisfy those wishing to be buried in sanctified ground. It is perhaps because of these territorial complications that many mixed-faith couples prefer to be cremated instead. Crematoria are owned by the local council, open to everyone, and the nature of the service is determined by the family request. It means that both partners can be cremated in the same place and their ashes are usually scattered under the same non-denominational rose bush.

There still remains the issue of who should take the service. Is it better for the minister of the person who died to do so, who can then conduct the last rites appropriate to the deceased? Or is it better for the minister of the spouse who survived to officiate, who can give fullest comfort to the partner left behind? In some cases, the choice can lead to odd results, as happened to one rabbi:

◆ I was asked to do the funeral of a Jew who had married a Methodist lady and I agreed to help. The problem was that on the day, there were about sixty people, and I realized that there were only two Jews present: the corpse and me! So I quickly altered my intended service and did most of the prayers in English so that it catered for the needs of the mourners.[4]

Ministers of most religions will officiate at the funeral service of someone who was not a member of their faith, but was married to a member. In fact, it often happens that if one partner did not have a strong faith of their own and joined in the religious activities of the other partner, that minister was the most appropriate person anyway. Mervyn, for instance, was a monthly churchgoer and his Sikh wife usually accompanied him, having lost contact with her own faith, although she never converted to Christianity. When she died, it seemed natural for the vicar to conduct her funeral as he knew her much better than any Sikh leader did.

In some instances, though, the different mourning rituals can leave an already devastated spouse feeling even more distraught. When Will died, his Jewish widow, Muriel, arranged the Catholic funeral she thought he would have wanted. Although this gave her some comfort, she felt very unhappy at the way in which it was conducted: the service seemed so alien to her, while references in the eulogy to her husband being 'reborn in the love of Christ' made her feel even more cut off from him. Louise had an even greater shock when she discovered that her Muslim husband – who had never been to a mosque in the thirty-seven years of their marriage – had left instructions in his will that his body was to be taken back to Pakistan. No doubt he wished to symbolically return to the land and faith of his forefathers, but it was ill-judged not to have prepared her for that moment in advance, and inconsiderate not to have discussed how that might affect her.

As in the case of children's religious education, those who coped with death best were those who had discussed matters well beforehand and taken acount of each other's feelings and preferences. Gavina, for example, assumed she would be cremated as is the Hindu tradition, whereas her Jewish husband felt strongly that he wished to be able to visit her grave and have a physical spot to go to. In the end, they agreed that she would be cremated but her ashes buried and a small tombstone erected. Exchanging simple information can also prove helpful as in the clash between customs over the coffin. In many Christian traditions, mourners are seated in the chapel and the coffin is brought in last, whereas the Jewish tradition is for the coffin to enter first and mourners to follow behind it. Moreover, the latter opt for wood that is of poor quality, so that there is no distinction between a rich and a poor man's coffin, while the former often have beautifully carved wood with ornate handles so as to best honour the deceased. Some couples decide that, as in their marriage ceremony, it would be wrong to have just one tradition represented and so ask the minister to include prayers and rituals from both faiths. Another option is to avoid the involvement of any ministers and to ask someone from the family to officiate or to approach the Humanist Association. The latter have experienced a major surge in such requests recently, partly from humanists who do not want any religious format, but also from mixed-faith couples who feel that a neutral approach is best suited to their circumstances.

Formulating a joint approach to death can be especially important if a mixed-faith couple are not saying goodbye to each other, but to a child that has died or been killed. At such times, parents can be overcome with a range of feelings, from anger to disbelief to guilt to despair. If their religious traditions conflict – cremation versus burial, women do or do not attend funerals, mourning is done alone or with the community – the pain can be even greater. When Ivy lost a baby through a cot-death, she wanted to have a photograph put on the stone. Her Muslim husband objected to a human image in a cemetery and said it felt pagan. Ivy, a Catholic, has resented that decision ever since and tends to visit the grave alone because it just leads to a row if the two of them go together. It means that her grief has an added layer of rage on top of it.

Notes

1 Christensen, Harold T., 'Failure in mixed marriages' in *Living Judaism*, Winter, 1968/9, p. 13; *Dovetail*, August 1995, p. 1

2 Bahr, Howard M., 'Religious Intermarriage and Divorce in Utah and the Mountain States' in *Journal for the Scientific Study of Religion*, Vol. 20 No. 3, September 1981, p. 251

3 UCLA study for the American Council on Education, Los Angeles, 1986

4 This was in fact the experience of the author on three occasions

Chapter Eight

Special cases

Ministers of religion who marry out – gays and lesbians
– mixed colour – the special relationship between
Catholics and Jews – enemies who become lovers –
same-faith marriages that become mixed-faith ones –
inter-church marriages – marriage between a believer
and an atheist

Every case of mixed-faith marriage is a special case, but some
are more special than others because of the particularly unusual
dimension they have. One of these is ministers of religion who
marry someone of a different faith to them. Unlike others, this
can present not only a personal challenge, but also a professional minefield. Ministers are supposed to embody the beliefs
they preach and are expected to bear witness to them through
their own life. They can appear to some congregants to have
gone severely astray if they choose to marry someone who does
not share that faith or whose own religion is even in direct
opposition to it. Derek is a vicar with a Hindu wife, but
although he has no problem with the multiplicity of gods she
worships and considers them different manifestations of the
one universal deity, he acknowledges that it took a while for
some of his flock to feel equally comfortable. Ralph has a
smaller theological divide between himself and his Jewish wife,
but tells of the hostility he has experienced from members of
his church and the difficulty in finding a job. His wife is still

expected to play a supporting role as the pastor's wife, which sometimes leads to difficulties of her own and feeling 'an identity crisis – if I am a Jew, what am I doing in church so much? I have learned to cope with silently chanting Jewish services in church when necessary.'[1] A female Christian minister faced a different problem when she chose to keep her first husband's surname rather than take that of her new husband when she remarried. He was Jewish and much as she loved him she felt it would be impossible professionally to take his surname: 'I don't want to be the Rev. Donna Goldstein.'[2] It would be impossible for a congregational rabbi in Britain to be married to a non-Jew, but in America the situation is different. In the relative tolerance of Colorado, a female rabbi with a Christian husband finds that 'My life has become a grand experiment, an experiment in learning to balance amongst the paradoxes. I use several laboratories: my congregation, my home and, most sensitive and bespattered, my heart.'[3] Of course, the couples in all these cases also see many advantages arising from their situation, both in terms of their love for each other and the extra insights it brings into their ministry. However, there is no uniform attitude to the question of the children's identity. For some, it is inevitable that they follow the faith of the minister in the family, as they largely attend his/her place of worship even though they also go to that of the other parent. For some, it is determined by other considerations. Jim is an Anglican priest but he and his wife decided the children would be Jewish – partly because Jewish identity is passed through the mother's line, and partly to prevent the loss of 'a small and historically vulnerable faith such as Judaism ... [and it becoming] an object of anthropological interest rather than a living reminder of a God who acts in history to create and liberate'.[4]

Variations on this theme include those who enter mixed-faith marriages who are the children of ministers. In addition to the potential problems already discussed earlier, two others arise. One is the sense of professional failure that the parent can feel, as did a rabbi whose eldest son chose a Christian wife and who felt 'it was a slap in the face for everything I stood for' (although the son saw it simply as finding a partner who loved and understood him and was shocked at his father's hurt). The second difficulty was for the father to face his congregation after years of preaching against intermarriage and urging parents to live committed Jewish lives so as to prevent their children marrying out of the faith. Now what could he tell them? He felt as if his credibility had been undermined and that no sermon would ever have the same authority that it once did. The same applies to a number of vicars whose sons and daughters have married members of other religions and caused raised eyebrows in the pews. One of those most hurt was a missionary priest who had spent most of the last thirty years converting others to Christianity and who was then horrified to find that his daughter was marrying an 'unbeliever'. In his eyes, she was joining the 'ranks of the devil' and calling his life's work into question.

An entirely different type of mixed marriages are those that are mixed-faith but same-sex. Gays and lesbians have long been used to prejudice and even persecution. When they 'come out' and reveal the true nature of their sexuality, the rejection can not only be from friends and work colleagues, but can be particularly fierce from members of their family. This is despite the fact that in the last thirty years homosexuality has become much more talked about publicly, is no longer illegal between consenting adults in private, and many parents are aware that there is approximately a 5–10% chance that a child of theirs might be homosexual. For some parents it is disgrace enough that their child is gay or lesbian, and the religious character of their partner is irrelevant. For others, it does matter. When Jackie's parents had recovered from the shock that their daughter was lesbian they hoped that 'if all else fails, perhaps I'll meet a nice Jewish girl'. It was not to be, and so 'they have had to accept a "double whammy" – that I'm in a relationship with a woman and that she's non-Jewish'. Their reactions typified the variant responses possible. Jackie's mother accepted the relationship and taught her partner, Linda, how to do Jewish cooking. In complete contrast, Linda's mother displayed her feelings when she died by cutting Linda out of her will in case Linda died and Jackie inherited her money.[5] Sharon and Annette obtained not only parental approval for their lesbian mixed-faith partnership but religious backing too. Their 'commitment ceremony' in California was attended by a large number of guests and conducted jointly by a pastor and a rabbi. A more difficult time was experienced by Guy, whose Church of Scotland father was apoplectic when he set up home with his Muslim lover Taki. One of the father's brothers was gay, so he was used to two men living together, but he felt that 'the clash of cultures turns the undesirable into the totally unacceptable'.

There are two other issues that confront mixed-faith gay couples. One is the reaction of the faiths themselves, with many being opposed to homosexuality. 'You shall not lie with a man as with a woman' declares the Bible,[6] while Leviticus 20:13 repeats the condemnation in even stronger terms and lays down the death penalty for all practitioners. Lesbianism is condemned too, but not so strongly, and has less of a stigma attached to it. The more liberal traditions within Christianity and Judaism reject the notion of homosexuality being a perversion and accept it as a natural condition for those born that way. However, many of those who are gay and religious still find the uncompromising stance of the sacred texts painful and feel hesitant about participating in the life of their community. When they are part of a mixed-faith relationship too, they can feel doubly isolated: condemned for not fitting into the faith properly and yet also condemned for choosing a partner from outside that faith. The second issue they face is that some of the family rituals are traditionally ascribed to members of one particular sex, and it may be the one that is missing in a same-sex family. In the Jewish home on a Friday night, for instance, it is the woman who lights the Sabbath candles and the man who says the blessings over the bread and wine. It is a matter of custom rather than law, so there is no reason why members of different sexes cannot swop roles – as happens in more liberal circles in heterosexual families – but having to break these traditional moulds emphasises the new practices that gay couples have to pioneer. If the other partner does not share that faith, and all roles have to be taken by just one partner, it can prove very lonely and can lead to dropping home ceremonies. For some, therefore, the result can be that religious participation becomes increasingly limited, both in the place of worship and in the home. As always, though, there is another side to the story and while those facing difficulties may be in the majority, other mixed-faith gay couples find the sharing of different religious traditions part of the joy of living together.

The case of Arnie is instructive here. His Baptist parents were appalled that he had a Muslim boyfriend with whom he shared a flat: 'It's bad enough you being gay,' they told him, 'but couldn't you have picked a white Christian boy?' It is almost certain that of the two adjectives, the truly important one for the parents was not 'Christian' but 'white'. A black Christian boy would have probably been equally unwelcome. As was seen in a previous chapter, it is clear that religious prejudice often masks, or goes hand-in-hand with, racial prejudice. A blatant example of this happened to Gary, whose parents strongly objected to his black lapsed Christian girlfriend, Dawn, when they first started dating. When he pressed them, they just said it was because she was not Jewish and it would be confusing for the children to be brought up in a mixed-faith household. After two years together, they decided to marry and at the same time Dawn, without any prompting from Gary, decided she felt sufficiently at home in Judaism to want to convert. When Gary told his parents they now need have no fears about a mixed-faith household, their continued antagonism was testimony to their real, albeit unspoken, racial objections. It is clear that many families, coloured as much as white ones, who are prepared unwillingly to put up with mixed-faith marriages draw the line at mixed-race ones too.

If history is anything to go by, another taboo should also be unions between Catholics and Jews. In previous centuries the former persecuted the latter with horrendous zeal, including priest-led riots, mass expulsions, burnings at the stake and the tyranny of the Spanish Inquisition. Yet today their respective descendants are intermarrying furiously, with the rate of Catholic-Jewish unions being several times higher than would be expected given the fact that both are small minorities in Britain and to even meet in the first place is relatively uncommon. One recent study suggested that as many as 26% of Jews who marry non-Jews chose Catholics as their partner.[7] It implies more than accidental mating, but a hidden magnetism between members of the two faiths that makes them gravitate towards each other. One reason may be that both religions are cultural identities as much as faiths, with home customs and personal rituals playing a significant role for each one. It means that each partner understands why such customs – however different – are important to the other. It is not so much a matter of believing, but of belonging; and even if the beliefs lapse, one is no less a member of the fraternity. Family tradition is valued, along with a lifelong sense of roots. The slogan 'Once a Catholic, always a Catholic' reflects the superiority of the bloodline over theology, and can be said equally of Jews. A second factor is that members of both faiths are used to being minorities, experiencing prejudice, and suffering verbal or physical abuse just for who they are. They are both accustomed to being viewed as 'different' by others and, in turn, share an outsider's view of society. This also means that marrying into another minority carries less danger of being swamped by the majority culture and less stigma of having 'sold out' to it. Most significantly, it enables them to maintain their distinctiveness and their right to be different. The end result is that despite the two faiths being radically different and sharing a history book filled with bloody pages, many of their members now feel at home with each other and can relate to each other's traditions and needs.

The Spanish Inquisition has long ceased to exist, but there are many examples of children of current enemies becoming lovers. Rahini is a Hindu born in Britain who fell in love with Onkar, who came over from the Punjab with his Sikh parents as a small boy. Their relationship earned the lukewarm approval of both families, but when it was discovered that his uncle had been one of the militant separatists involved in the siege of the Amritsar Temple, her family said they would disown her if the marriage proceeded. Ronnie faced similar antagonism from his Jewish parents when he told them about his new girlfriend Helga, a German Lutheran. The reaction bordered on the hysterical, with accusations that he was trampling on the memory of the six million Jews murdered in the Holocaust and dark warnings about 'How can you sleep in peace next to someone when you can never be sure what her father did in the war?' In the event they did marry, and were rehabilitated in his family's eyes thanks to some inverted prejudice on the part of his grandmother. When she met Helga, she declared her approval – being swayed by the fact that Helga was tall and blonde, and had the same aristocratic bearing that the grandmother herself enjoyed and which she prized more highly than religion. Less easy to reconcile was the position of Edgar, who was the child of a German Christian father and German Jewish mother. They divorced when he was twelve and shortly before the war she brought Edgar to England where they built a new life for themselves. Years later he met up with his father again, but when asked he refused to talk about his wartime experiences. Edgar's double legacy was filled with religious, national and moral confusion: with which parent should he identify, the one who was amongst the victims or the one who was amongst the persecutors? Another crisis was provoked by Georgina, whose Jewish parents regularly visit Israel and strongly identify with the state. When she brought home Yousef, who was not only Muslim but an active supporter of the Palestinian cause, the Middle East conflict was transported to their front living-room. Georgina tried to argue that whatever the rights and wrongs being fought out across the Mediterranean, it should not be allowed to affect their relationship. However, neither her parents nor Yousef agreed and the ferocity of the argument was such that she cannot remember whether he walked out or they asked him to leave. Either way, it was an example of love not being able to conquer all.

Catholics and Protestants in Northern Ireland are well aware of the battle-lines that can turn religious differences into a matter of life and death. Same-faith marriages are the norm and account for approximately 90% of marriages. Those who fall in love across the sectarian divide face more than the usual complications of a mixed-faith marriage. When she was first dating Patrick, Geraldine did not tell her Protestant parents his name in case it gave away his Catholic roots. When planning their wedding they not only had to debate under which church's auspices they would be married – a difficult enough task in itself – but they also had to pay great attention to the location of the church: was it in an area of Belfast to which it was safe for relatives from both families to travel? A few years later they then faced the problem that a high percentage of schools in the province are denominational ones, and so even though they had wanted to keep both traditions open to their children, they were forced to make a choice as to which faith they would be enrolled in. Trish and James split up eighteen months into their courtship because they found the family pressures too great. 'Every time we sat down for dinner at home,' James said, 'I always got "You still seeing that Taig?" It just became too much.' In fact they later started seeing each other again and are now married with a seven-year-old daughter. She has inherited some of their problems and was found crying her eyes out because a school friend had told her that her father would go to hell because he was a Protestant. Other couples have had to contend with physical intimidation: Terry was beaten up at college whilst dating a Catholic girl and, in case he was unsure of the lesson he was supposed to learn, had the words 'Pope-lover' sprayed on his car. A husband and wife who were both doctors and who went to live in a small town found that they were judged not by their professional ability but by their mixed-faith marriage. Eventually silent hints of disapproval, along with some not-so-silent ones, proved too much and they returned to the relative anonymity of city life. Moreover, the problems that arise are not necessarily only from other people. The decision as to which church to attend and children's upbringing can lead to tension, while certain topics of conversation may have to be avoided if marital harmony is to be preserved. As Simon said: 'I've learnt that if I want to have a hot supper, I'd better not go on about the Pope while she's cooking.' The friction between the two communities also means that people have often absorbed much more prejudice against each other than they realize. Kim has been happily married to a Protestant for nine years, but having mixed almost exclusively in Catholic circles beforehand she still feels uneasy with some of his friends: 'There's a Prod mentality to them all which means I'm always on my guard somehow.' When such prejudices surface between the couple themselves, it can prove very damaging.

There are some couples who face a situation that has not been mentioned so far and which they themselves never even dreamt about. They are couples who both come from the same religious background but then find that this changes during the course of their marriage; their same-faith home becomes a mixed-faith one. There are two different ways in which this occurs. One is accidental, and tends to follow the pattern in Jane's story:

◆ My mother was the daughter of a Jewish woman who had married a Christian in 1911 and had been cut off from her family as a result. The children were not brought up Jewish and never knew she was Jewish. My mother was a nominal Christian but thought it natural that she would be married in church, as did I when it was my wedding. It was only when my mother died and we went through the family papers that we found out about my grandmother – which meant that I was Jewish too. It was a bit of a shock to my husband, although to me it made sense as I had never felt comfortable with Christianity and had always been interested in Jewish things – although never imagining it was actually my own heritage. I started reading Jewish books and after a while plucked up courage to go to a synagogue. Since then I've become thoroughly immersed in it all, although I do have to be careful not to overdo it in case my husband becomes resentful of the time I spend 'over at the Jewish place'.

Others discover their true roots from documents that surface during a house move, or from a chance remark from a distant relative, as when Jack's great-uncle was visiting him from Australia and revealed that far from being of ancient Church of England stock, the family had been Catholics three generations ago. In all cases, there is the personal shock at realizing one's religious history is different from that taken for granted all one's life. For some, it makes no real difference and is merely of historical interest, but many are affected by the knowledge and it can often lead to a new religious journey. In such cases, the effect is also felt by one's partner and any children, with their reactions ranging from support to indifference to displeasure. Like Jane's husband they may feel annoyed that the person they married had seemed to change their religious spots without any warning.

The other scenario is when one of the originally same-faith marriage partners decides to convert to another religion. Sally and John were both Presbyterians but lacked any real religious conviction and let religious life lapse save for weddings and funerals. After twenty-three years of marriage, Sally began to feel she needed a spiritual element to her life, became interested in Islam through a friend and joined a conversion class. On one level, John had no objections and was pleased she had found something that answered her needs; but he was worried that it might draw them apart and harm the otherwise successful marriage. For her part, Sally was very conscious that she could not participate as fully as she would like in local Muslim communal life without her husband, while she knew that she could not introduce home customs without antagonizing him. Both felt torn by separate conflicting needs, and the relationship underwent a difficult period before they managed to adjust to their new status as a mixed-faith couple. At least they did not have to worry about the children's education, as the two boys were already in their late teens when Sally changed faith. Rory and Helen did face that problem when, six years after having their twin sons baptized into the Catholic church, Rory decided to become a Buddhist. Helen was determined to continue the boys' Christian identity, but felt increasingly uncomfortable taking them to church alone. Rory was not opposed to this, but wanted to broaden their religious education to include Buddhism and to appreciate what it had to offer. Some fierce arguments resulted, with Helen accusing him of betraying his marriage vows to be a good Catholic husband and father, while he felt she no longer understood him. In the end, Helen gave way, although partly because she feared that, no longer being a Catholic, he might be more willing to initiate a divorce if she alienated him too much. There are also cases in which the religious balance of a marriage changes for the opposite reason – that a convert reverts to their original faith. George is one of those to whom this has happened. Born a Hindu, he converted to Christianity when he was seventeen and several years later met his wife, who came from a staunchly evangelical Christian family. After eleven years of marriage he began to feel less at home in Christianity, and a longing for his ancestral faith. His wife was worried by the increasing number of Hindu books he read and her worst fears were confirmed when he announced he wanted to return to Hinduism. She felt abandoned both as a Christian who took her faith very seriously, and as a wife and mother who was now the only adult Christian in the marriage. After a few years, the strain proved too much and they went their separate ways.

There are some mixed-faith marriages that to outsiders may not appear to be mixed-faith, but certainly do to insiders. Amongst these are marriages between Catholics and Protestants in England, who are supposedly members of the same Christian family, but for whom the differences can sometimes make family life seem very fraught indeed. Many of the usual issues surface: In whose place of worship will the couple marry? How will irate parents be pacified? Which identity will the children adopt? What traditions will be kept up at home? In some aspects, the question marks are not as far-ranging as they are for others: if a baby boy is born the debate is not whether to circumcise him or baptize him, but which sort of baptism to have. In other ways, there are special problems: children in other mixed-faith marriages who are being brought up in the religion of both parents can accompany one to synagogue on Saturday and the other to church on Sunday; but children of inter-church families have to choose which parent to go to church with if the service times clash. A compromise adopted by many couples is to go to each other's church on alternate Sundays. The theological gulf between the two branches of Christianity is made all the wider because it affects not just matters of belief, but practical issues. The Catholic authorities, for example, do not allow Protestants to take communion in their churches. This can present major problems for a religiously committed couple when attending Catholic worship together, who find they are then divided at the most important part of the service. As one Roman Catholic remarked sadly: 'The longest walk I ever take is up to the altar – while my wife has to stay behind.'[8] It also means that if their children have not been baptized in the Catholic Church, they too are excluded from participating fully in one parent's place of worship. As in other cases, children can often reconcile these discrepancies better than parents, and they are not worried by the different style of services. For them it is not a case of Protestant versus Catholic, but of the 'Ay-men' church and the 'Ah-men' one. Much depends on the attitude of the minister in the local church, with reports of some being enormously helpful to inter-church families, while others were highly insensitive, making one partner feel 'a second class Christian who was not particularly welcome'. An Anglican woman recalls how she was invited to join the church widows' circle after attending services for a year with only her daughters, to which she gave the price-less reply: 'My husband's not dead – he's just Roman Catholic.'[9] It is a painful irony that those being rejected are precisely those who value their Christian faith most dearly, as in the story of the Church of England father who was refused communion at the altar rails at a Catholic Mass, when his own son was standing by the priest and holding the communion plate.

Many inter-church couples feel aggrieved that their deep faith and sincerity is being ignored because they belong to 'the wrong branch of what should be a united faith'. In their eyes, the real problem is not that there are inter-church marriages but that there are inter-church divisions. In fact, they often see them-selves as having the lonely but prophetic mission of showing through their own lives how to heal the breaches within the Church.

◆ We don't think that our situation as inter-church families is a problem. We live it as an opportunity. An opportunity for each of us to rediscover our own faith … to work out what is important in the customs and traditions of our own Church … to move beyond prejudices … to live in faith beyond the routine of our own certain-ties … to see our children feel at home in both Churches … to go beyond the rules … to help our Churches forward.[10]

In this respect they were much encouraged by the words of Pope John Paul II during his visit to England in May 1982, when he commented on their unique role at a speech in York: 'You live in your marriage the hopes and difficulties of the path to Christian unity.' In the years since then, many couples have wished that the Churches would ease their lot by moves towards reconciliation, and transform the strains of 'double belonging' into a reciprocal sharing.

A different set of problems is experienced by those couples who are not so much in mixed-faith marriages as in unions in which only one partner has a faith and the other is either no-faith or anti-faith. In both instances the spouse with a faith can feel a lack of support, while the other can resent the occasions when religion impinges on their lives. Jeff is a convinced atheist and can list a catalogue of grievances against his Methodist wife:

◆ Don't get me wrong, we have a good marriage and I think the world of her. But every marriage has its sore spots and, for me, it's Val and the church. It means her going off to services, or having the ladies' circle committee meetings here every now and then, or wanting to visit Christian sites when on holiday and all I want to do is stay on the beach.

Similar flashpoints in other families arise over religious traditions within the home – whether lighting candles, having special symbols on the wall, and eating or avoiding certain foods. Agreeing a common policy regarding the children can be as difficult as in a mixed-faith family. Jeff and Val's compromise was to let their five- and seven-year-old daughters 'decide for themselves if they wanted to go with Mummy to church on Sundays or fishing with Daddy, and present it as a choice between two hobbies'. It is an apt description, because although ministers of all faiths would be loathe to describe religion in such subjective and take-it-or-leave-it terms, for those in mixed-faith marriages religion has become a matter of individual preference, and certainly not to be imposed on the other partner if it would harm their relationship.

Notes

1 Blank, Emily and Gonichelis, Ralph, 'The Joys and Pitfalls of Intermarriage When One Partner Is a Pastor' in *Dovetail*, Missouri, Vol. 2 No. 5, April/May 1994, p. 4

2 Schafer, Donna E., 'When a Clergyperson Marries Someone of a Different Faith' in *Dovetail*, ibid., p. 2

3 Firestone, Tirzah, 'When a Clergyperson Marries Someone of a Different Faith' in *Dovetail*, ibid., p. 3

4 Newell, Christopher, 'A decision to celebrate diversity', in *Church Times*, London, 26 July 1991

5 *New Moon*, London, January 1993, p. 35

6 Leviticus 18:22

7 Survey at the Sternberg Centre for Judaism, London, 1988

8 quoted in Heron, Alasdair, *Two Churches, One Love*, Dublin, APCK, 1977, p. 79

9 quoted in 'Interchurch Families: Ecumenism with a human face' in *Centrepiece*, No. 19 issued by Association of Inter-church Families, London, 1988

10 Eric Lombard quoted in *Inter-church Families*, Vol. 2 No. 1, London, January 1994, p. 7

Chapter Nine

The balance sheet

The four myths surrounding mixed-faith marriages –
the different types of such marriages – their overall effect
– and the challenge they present to the religious
authorities in Britain

Until now there have been four assumptions that were widely held about mixed-faith marriages. They have been common currency for decades, arising from false judgments that were either made in ignorance or were based on some true cases which were mistakenly taken as representative of all cases. It must also be said that these assumptions were often encouraged by ministers of all faiths as a way of reinforcing their dire warnings against the perils of intermarriage. The numerous cases examined in this book have exposed these assumptions as myths. They are not only untrue, but mislead religious leaders who are trying to formulate a response to the growing number of mixed-faith couples.

The first myth is that those who marry out of their faith are deliberately rejecting that faith. They are not. Many would have been more than happy to marry a co-religionist, but it just so happened that the person they met and with whom they fell in love was of a different religion. They still have a deep attachment to their faith, with strong emotional ties that will remain with them for the rest of their life. For them, marrying out does not mean opting out. They still wish to observe their faith, be part of the religious community to which they belong, and pass on that heritage to their children. The question mark is very often not with them, but with the religious establishment and whether it will permit them to remain a member of it. As Noreen said: 'Just because I have fallen in love with someone who is not a Muslim, it does not make me any less of a Muslim. I will always identify with Islam – now it's up to Islam whether it wants to identify with me.'

The second myth is that those who marry out of their faith are only ones who have not received any formal religious instruction or have not experienced any home celebrations from their parents; in other words, intermarriage only affects the nominal members and not the educated ones. It is certainly true that the less religious background a person has, the less they consider it a criterion when selecting a partner. However, there are many who had both a firm and positive religious background yet who also find happiness with a partner from a different faith. They enjoyed, and are grateful for, a vibrant family religious life and they attended after-school classes or even a religious day school. Most are not headstrong young-sters who rush into marriage blindly. They are often mature and experienced adults who had given much thought to their situation before making a decision. Moreover, they had assumed they would marry within their faith, until circum-stances introduced them to the person with whom they wanted to spend the rest of their life. If they are judged by their religious knowledge and identity, then their upbringing was highly successful; if they are judged by their choice of marriage partner, then it was an abject failure. Much depends on the yardstick that is used.

The third myth is that mixed-faith marriages are doomed to fail. Some do end in tears and there is evidence that such couples have a somewhat higher rate of divorce than do same-faith couples. However, the latter also have a high divorce rate and the argument is not whether mixed-faith couples get divorced and same-faith couples do not; both do and the debate is over percentages. The notion that 'the family that prays together, stays together' is no longer true. For many people, religion has become privatized. It is the individual hobby of a particular member of the family – which need not be shared by other members and does not affect their overall cohesion. Family or clergy opposed to intermarriage who preach that divorce is likely and that unhappiness is guaranteed are both distorting the truth and undermining their own message; it is all too easy to point to mixed-faith couples who have shared a long and happy life together.

The fourth myth is that mixed-faith marriage is an issue restricted to certain religions or certain denominations within them. Statements often thrown around in conversation – such as 'Catholics always stick with their own' or 'Jews only mix amongst themselves' – are ridiculous when compared to the enormous outmarriage rate of the former and the rising one of the latter. Equally unsound is the supposition that members of recent immigrant faiths only marry amongst themselves, whereas Hindus, Muslims and Sikhs are changing their traditional marriage patterns rapidly. It is also assumed that the more liberal branches of the faiths are more prone to intermarriage. This is an allegation that is usually part of internal fights within those faiths, with more traditional groups throwing at the liberal ones what they consider to be the worst possible accusation: encouraging assimilation and allowing adherents to kill off their faith without noticing it. In fact, it is clear that mixed-faith marriages are prevalent amongst all sections of each faith. Amongst the most documented of the religions in terms of mixed-faith marriages, Judaism, it is apparent that the issue affects Orthodox communities as much as Reform ones, and seminars for Jews in mixed-faith marriages attract equal numbers from both camps.[1]

It is clear from the above that those in mixed-faith marriages cannot be stereotyped. It also means that they cannot be conveniently categorized for dismissive remarks or quick-fit solutions. They vary enormously and those concerned with the issue – be it from a religious, counselling or sociological point of view – must acknowledge the diversity of factors and results. At least ten different types of relationships can be analysed, and no doubt other commentators will be able to suggest further ones:

1 *Dual faith harmonious.* Both partners have their own strong faith, respect each other's religious needs and are mutually supportive.
2 *Dual faith conflicting.* Both partners have their own strong faith, but find it a source of tension and rivalry.
3 *Single faith harmonious.* One partner has a strong faith and the other does not, but is happy to be supportive.
4 *Single faith conflicting.* One partner has a strong faith and the other does not, and resents the intrusion of religion in the marriage.
5 *Merged faith.* Both partners decide to merge their two faiths into a set of beliefs and way of life that they can share.
6 *Alternative faith.* Both partners agree to adopt a third faith, to which they can both belong and feel at ease.
7 *Lapsed faith.* Neither partner values their religious traditions and they share a common 'lapsedness'.
8 *Converted same-faith.* One partner has converted to the faith of the other, whether before or after marriage, but still carries vestiges of the former faith, including close relatives who are part of the other faith.
9 *Re-emerged mixed-faith.* One partner, usually previously lapsed, has felt a re-emergence of their religious roots and thereby changes the religious balance of the marriage.
10 *Confused faith.* Both partners have religious traditions of their own, but are not sure what they believe and go through periods of making a religious effort, jointly or separately, and then giving it up.

The combined effect of these different types of mixed-faith marriages is profound and is having an impact on a wide range of areas. One is the level of religiosity of the couple themselves. An earlier chapter had presented a bleak outlook, with 49% of Christian-Jewish couples in America belonging neither to a church nor to a synagogue. Figures for actual attendance rate at a place of worship also showed a low level of participation:[2]

	Never attend	Few times a year	Once a month or more
Church	49%	40%	11%
Synagogue	34%	57%	9%

The religious involvement of children of mixed-faith marriages was also seen to decrease. It is inevitable that in those homes in which religion is not valued – or valued but deliberately suppressed in order not to cause conflict – that the religious life of both parents and children wanes considerably. However, two caveats should be borne in mind which prevent the endorsement of the simple formula 'marrying out means dropping out'. First, the level of religious intensity among same-faith couples is also low. Countless churches throughout Britain are surrounded by Christian-Christian couples who never attend and have an extremely poor religious knowledge. In this respect, mixed-faith couples are part of a general trend towards religious indifference. As one vicar said sadly: 'I represent a minority faith in Britain and feel overwhelmed by the forces of secularism around me.'

The second caveat is that this trend may be prevalent amongst mixed-faith marriages but it is not universal. An astonishing but oft-quoted comment by a number of couples is that being in a mixed-faith relationship has strengthened rather than weakened their religious feelings, and it has led them to increase their knowledge and observances. As Rajiv explained:

◆ If I had married another Hindu who was like me, nominally attached to my religion but more interested in the outside world and what it had to offer, then I doubt we would have kept much tradition and would have become even more secular. But when I married Corinne, who is a Methodist, I realized that it would now be all too easy for Hinduism just to peter out, because she does not know it and it was up to me whether it died or survived in my family. I didn't suddenly become fanatical, but I did start making an effort to do things I wouldn't normally have done, so that I kept the flag flying and gave something for my children to relate to.

Beth felt exactly the same from a different perspective:

◆ You may not believe this, but I feel that being in a mixed marriage has made me more Jewish. With another Jew I would hardly have bothered with Jewish life, as we would both take it for granted as a cultural background. Now I have to take my religious heritage more seriously as it stands or falls by me. As a result I go to synagogue occasionally and attend adult education classes. In fact I am more involved than my sister who married another Jew and who only goes once a year. I've become the religious one in the family!

While priests, imams and rabbis will be delighted to hear such testimonies, they will probably be right in regarding them as representing a minority of those who marry someone of a different faith. They may be a significant minority and to be valued, but they do not compensate for the larger number lost to the respective faiths.

Another effect that is very evident to clergy is the financial consequences that can arise from the lesser commitment of many in mixed-faith marriages. It is not just a matter of having fewer worshippers, but also of having fewer contributors to support communal needs. The drop in offerings for church collection plates on Sunday mornings places even greater strain on the remaining congregants to pay for the upkeep of large buildings and ministers' stipends. The decrease in subscriptions to Jewish charities places similar pressures on agencies assisting Jewish old age homes and a network of other support groups, who now depend on a numerically smaller community and one which itself is ageing more and earning less. Figures from America show the marked contrast in giving patterns:

Donations to:	Both Jewish and general charities	Only Jewish charities	Only general charities	No charity
Same-faith couples	62.0%	13.3%	14.6%	10.1%
Mixed-faith couples	29.2%	4.1%	40.3%	26.4%

Thus donations purely to internal Jewish charities dropped by over two-thirds among mixed-faith couples, while those giving to both Jewish and general ones declined by over a half, with most of that deficit going to general charities. While no rabbi would have anything but praise for the marvellous and life-saving work often done by general charities, they would also be alarmed at the shortfall experienced by equally worthwhile charities working within the Jewish community. It is perhaps inevitable that all those in mixed-faith marriages who have to take account of two religious and cultural traditions will either try to support both – and therefore give less to each – or they will transfer loyalty from causes relating to neither faith in particular and concentrate on general causes which can appeal to both partners without generating any controversy between the two of them. This will also apply to work done for fellow congregants abroad, such as Christian missions in Africa, or fund-raising for Israel, or supporting Catholic hospices, or sending money to Muslim charities in countries from where one's parents or grandparents had originated. In all these cases, the decrease in contributions is partly the result of sidestepping potential arguments over domestic finances, and partly a lessening in identification by each of the mixed-faith partners with those from their own backgrounds. If having separate roots is sensed to be divisive by a mixed-faith couple, the most natural solution for them is to forge a new identity that emphasizes what they have in common and distances them from previous loyalties.

There are some voices of optimism amid the gloom. They claim that when a Muslim or a Catholic or Jew marry someone of a different faith, they are not detracting from their number but adding to it. For them, intermarriage is not a catastrophe but a source of recruitment. In a similar vein, when a child of, for instance, a Presbyterian-Hindu marriage is asked his religious identity and says that he is 'half and half', the optimists would regard this not as a sign of confusion but of double belonging. The evidence seems to suggest that the view is either a case of self-deception or, more charitably, an overdose of wishful thinking. While there are many mixed-faith families whose lives do justify such optimism, a larger proportion support the prophets of religious doom.

In some respects the prophets have an easy time. They may be reviled and persecuted, but they can at least hurl down invective from the mountain tops and then stomp off into the desert. It is the clergy who stay behind to pick up the pieces and who must now face the reality of mixed-faith marriages as a major phenomenon in Britain. Until now, all that has been devoted to the issue by the religious hierarchies are a few sermons and the occasional working party. Henceforth ministers of all faiths will have to both acknowledge the new religious landscape and formulate a response to it. In judging how to react, they will have to take into account the two key findings that have become apparent regarding mixed-faith marriages. Firstly, that it is a trend that is dependent on so many factors in society at large, that it is futile to think that a few more sermons can halt it. Continuing the condemnation is certainly an option, but one likely to yield little result. Ministers must come to terms with the lack of power that they exercise in this respect. There is every reason to assume that the trend will remain and grow, and unless ministers wish to get their feet wet they should avoid becoming ecclesiastical Canutes. The clear implication is that the only successful response will be one that is positive and that seeks to work *with* mixed-faith couples rather than *against* them. This is reinforced by the second finding, that many within mixed-faith marriages still value their religious roots and wish to maintain contact with their faith-community. Here is where the real power of the clergy lies. By being welcoming to both partners, they can play a major role in influencing whether that residual loyalty is developed or jettisoned. Some ministers may find it difficult to welcome those who, according to one interpretation, have 'betrayed' their religious past. They may find it even more distasteful to welcome the other-religion partner. Moreover, it may provoke a crisis of conscience to welcome their children in the knowledge that they are being brought up in both faiths, or even the other one. However, unless such policy changes and leaps of religious imagination are made, ministers will find their flock dwindling and will see a growing number of former congregants occupying a religious no-man's-land. The coming decades will offer a unique opportunity to relate to the faith of the mixed-faith couples that can be seized or squandered.

It is a path that will involve much soul-searching for the clergy, partly because it contradicts long-standing traditions for many of them, and partly because it seems to bring into conflict two values – faith and family – which had always appeared to be synonymous in the past. A new theological paradigm will have to be constructed by them that still upholds the ideal of same-faith marriages, but gives equal validity to mixed-faith ones. The concept of diversity within the family will have to be given a place in the religious spectrum, so that the spiritual expressions of partners can differ from each other without calling into question the sincerity of either one or the legitimacy of the relationship. The shift in thinking needed applies to virtually all the faiths in Britain, although perhaps most urgently of all to Hinduism, Islam and Sikhism, if they are to cope adequately with the explosion in the intermarriage rate that is expected in their midst in particular. The other faiths have much to re-evaluate too, but at least have a greater experience of the issue with which to temper their approach. All ministers who wish to remain in touch with their members will be obliged to walk a theological tightrope: not wanting to encourage relationships that may endanger their faith and add to the many potential hazards surrounding the institution of marriage; yet wishing to give pastoral support to those in such relationships and to nurture the religious feelings they still possess. Beneath that tightrope lies the deep chasm between theology and reality that exists in so many people's lives. It is epitomized by the question of David who said: 'I am religious, I have met someone special and I have a choice – do I remain single and unhappy, or do I marry someone who loves me, cares for me and is not of my faith?' David's question is being answered in practice by countless individuals like him who decide for themselves to follow the latter course; but the religious answer which he and they would welcome is either avoided or put in a hostile and negative fashion. The time is already overdue for the major faiths to answer David's question directly and helpfully – or else risk that he ceases to involve the rest of his life, and that of his children, with them any further. Mixed-faith marriages may be a challenge for every couple involved, but they are also proving the greatest challenge facing the major religions as the power of human emotions turns dogmas into confetti and bakes a joint wedding cake out of different religious ingredients.

Notes

1 Romain, Jonathan, 'How Can a Jew Remain a Jew?' in *Manna*, Autumn 1989, London, p. 18; Schmool, Marlena, 'Analysis of

Participants at Intermarriage Seminar January 1990' unpublished report, London, Board of Deputies Community Research Unit, 1990
2 Mayer, Egon, *1990 National Jewish Population Survey,* New York, Council of Jewish Federations, 1991

Appendix 1

Questions for mixed-faith couples to ask themselves

The following checklist may help mixed-faith couples clarify some of the issues that face them. The first section is relevant to all concerned – whether they have just entered the relationship or have been together for many years. The second section applies to particular stages of one's life.

Relationships
1 What is important to me about my religious background, memories, community, beliefs and customs?
2 Have I discussed them fully with my partner?
3 How much is he/she able to accommodate them?
4 Do I know what is important religiously for my partner?
5 How will I fit in with them?
6 Have I discussed my view of the relationship with my family (and given them a chance to express their feelings)?
7 Have I discussed my view of the relationship with my partner's family (and given them a chance to express their feelings?)

8 Am I aware that the needs and attitudes of either one of us may change over the years, and am I prepared to work around that?

Special Issues

9 What will happen on the wedding day?

10 What home ceremonies and symbols will we have?

11 What will happen on major festivals?

12 In what religious activities outside the home will we participate – either separately or together?

13 What role will our respective families play in our life?

14 What will we do about the religious identity of children?

15 What will we do about the religious education of children?

16 What initiation ceremonies will we have for them?

17 Will the grandparents play a role in the children's religious life?

18 What funeral arrangements do we want?

Two golden rules

1 Discuss in advance all the issues that are likely to arise.

2 Keep the channels of communication open with family.

Appendix 2

Useful organizations for mixed-faith couples

❖

The following organizations offer a variety of services that may be of use to couples in, or about to enter mixed-faith relationships. Please note that the details are correct at the time of publication, but may change thereafter.

Asian Family Counselling Service. 74 The Avenue, Ealing, London W13 8LB Tel. 0181 997 5749

Association of Inter-church Families. Inter-Church House, 35–41 Lower Marsh, London SE1 7RL Tel. 0171 620 4444

Catholic Marriage Advisory Council. Clitherow House, 1 Blythe Mews, London W14 0NW Tel. 0171 371 1341

Council of Christians and Jews. 1 Dennington Park Road, London NW6 1AX Tel. 0171 794 8178

Inter-Faith Network. 5–7 Tavistock Place, London WC1H 9SS Tel. 0171 388 0008

Jewish Marriage Council. 23 Ravenshurst Avenue, London NW4 4EE Tel. 0181 203 6311

Network (self-support group for mixed-faith couples). c/o

Community Outreach, The Sternberg Centre for Judaism, 80 East End Road, London N3 2SY Tel. 0181 349 4731

One Plus One (marriage and partnership research charity). 12 New Burlington Street, London W1X 1FF Tel. 0171 734 2020

People in Harmony (self-support group for mixed-race relationships). 49 Ledgers Road, Slough, Berks SL1 2RQ Tel. 01753 552559

Relate. Herbert Gray College, Little Church Street, Rugby CV21 3AP Tel. 01788 573241

Further reading

❖

The following is a list of publications relating to the subject of mixed-faith marriage *in addition* to those already quoted in the notes at the end of each chapter.

Books

Alibhai-Brown, Yasmin and Montague, Anne, *The Colour of Love: Mixed-Race Relationships,* London, Virago Press, 1992

Band, Mary, *Whom God Hath Joined,* Essex, McCrimmons, 1987

Kilcourse, George, *Double Belonging: Inter-church Families and Christian Unity,* New York, Paulist Press, 1992

Modood, Tariq, Beishon, Sharon and Virdee, Satnam, *Changing Ethnic Identities,* London, Policy Studies Institute, 1994

Romain, Jonathan, *Faith and Practice: A Guide to Reform Judaism Today,* London, Reform Synagogues of Great Britain, 1991

Seltzer, Sanford, *Jews and Non-Jews: Getting Married,* New York, Union of American Hebrew Congregations, 1984

Articles

Ahsan, Manazir, 'The Muslim Family in Britain' in *God's Law Versus State Law*, ed. King, Michael, London, Grey Seal, 1995

Clulow, Christopher, 'Marriage across frontiers: national, ethnic and religious differences in partnership', London, *Journal of Family Therapy*, Vol. 8 No. 1, 1993

Cohen, Nina, 'Same or different? A problem of identity in cross-cultural marriages', London, *Journal of Family Therapy*, Vol. 4, 1982

Lamb, Christopher, 'Mixed-Faith Marriage: A Case for Care' in *Love the Stranger*, Hooker, R. and Lamb, C., London, SPCK, 1986

Schmool, Marlena, 'Synagogue Marriages in Britain in the 1980s', London, *The Jewish Journal of Sociology* (Vol. XXXIII No. 2), December 1991

Pamphlets and Reports

Getting Married? One Partner Roman Catholic, The Other Not? London, Association of Inter-church Families, 1988

Marrying A Catholic? London, Catholic Marriage Advisory Council, 1985

Romain, Jonathan, *I'm Jewish, My Partner Isn't*, London, Reform Synagogues of Great Britain, 1993

Wilcock, Evelyn, *The Half-Jew and the Synagogue: Jewish Failure or Jewish Future*, London, published by the author, 1990

Willson, Jane Wynne, *Funerals without God: A Practical Guide to Non-religious Funerals*, London, British Humanist Association, 1989